WHO IS THIS BOOK FOR?

To benefit from this book, you need to have awareness, be open to opportunities and take action. You need to be someone who wants to take a fresh approach to business during your entrepreneurial journey. You could be:

- An entrepreneur;
- Working in sales/marketing;
- Wanting to start a business;
- Been in business for three years and turning over up to £1 million;
- In a job and looking for a second income;
- An action-orientated individual;
- People who want to make a difference and are passionate about it.

This book is not for you if:

- You pick things up and never finish them;
- You skim read books and go to one chapter middle way through the book because you think you know what the first chapter is going to tell you;
- You've spent your time/money working with an agency to build your online presence and it's worked for you.

The practical benefits this book will give you are:

- Breaking old habits and building new ones;
- Building blocks for a 21st century business;
- Learning how to use technology to grow your business through sales and marketing;
- Having the confidence to share your business online, knowing it will solve your target customers' pain.

If you keep doing what you're doing and keep getting the same results, you need to stop and take a fresh approach. Everything I share with you in this book is based on real life examples myself or my clients have personally experienced. To really benefit from what this book has to offer, read from the beginning to the end logically. This book is not going to help you if read Chapter One and jump straight to Chapter Six. You need to understand why you're doing what you're doing progressively to take away the full message of this incredibly practical and hands-on workbook.

"Sending a random tweet or uploading a photo once a month to Facebook is not enough social media activity for a successful business. For every action or no action there is a reaction.
You must always ask yourself: what is the outcome I am seeking to get the result I am looking for?"

WHAT OTHERS SAY

"Marketing is not a standalone activity and this book takes business owners very effectively through all of the aspects of a company that need to be considered to build a great marketing strategy. Warren reminds us that for marketing to be effective, the business must be in a good shape first. Far more than just theory, he provides practical step-by-step actions and tools to implement. It is a great guide for any business owner."
COO, Joanna Hill, *Start Up Loans.*

"Warren Knight has shared not only his extensive research - and what a resource that is - but his personal experience in this latest book on digital marketing. He holds nothing back in his bid to offer help to both the new and growing entrepreneur."
Guy Clapperton, Author, *This Is Social Media.*

"Think Digital First gives you real Digital Marketing strategies for real businesses who want to create real success."
Ryan Pinnick, CEO of *Natural Success.*

"Having known Warren for 20 years I can say he is a true entrepreneur. Warren has definitely found his home in the digital sector. Identifying opportunities and taking on challenges he is adaptable and sharp minded. Warren has shown that he is adept at integrating and most importantly creating value for his clients.I highly recommend that you invest in his book; Think #Digital First on your journey to greater success in the digital sphere and your life."
Karl Pearsall; *YesGroup* worldwide founder, Branding Expert, Entrepreneur and Author.

"Must Read - brilliant new socially-savvy business and social media guidebook for entrepreneurs; start-ups and business owners. This very readable, energetic and powerful book is well-structured and each chapter builds your understanding and knowledge, enabling you to implement the strategies he recommends to build your business, your customers and your followers. Warren provides a step-by-step process to improve your business mind set and build your framework for success. He shares the latest tools and technology; well-illustrated with excellent graphics, lists and dot points that are easy to follow. My recommendation is to put your order for a copy of the book in now on his website before you miss out!"

Wendy Yorke; Cross Cultural, Diversity & Inclusion Trainer, Author & Performance and Book Coach.

"Most businesses invest a lot of time and money in a marketing strategy but without the strategy, and then wonder why the results are poor. Warren has had much success helping ambitious companies fill that void, and he has laid it all down within his excellent book for the modern entrepreneur."

Daryl Woodhouse, Founder & Executive Chairman,
Advantage Business Partnerships Ltd.

*"**Think #Digital First is my #NBF!!** As usual, Warren has delivered above and beyond and given those of us who run a SME an essential, **easy to understand 'work-book'** packed full of cutting edge digital information, that when implemented 'consistently' will help your business soar online. This is the only book you'll need in 2015 to help you grow your business online. Thank you Warren for making this digital journey way more easy to navigate for us NON-technical people!! Love it! #BuyItNow!!"*

Andrea Littlefair, International Business Owner.

"From start to finish "Think Digital First" grounded my ideals on business life in the digital age. This book allowed me to reposition my thought process, think outside of my current box, and strip everything back to basics, whilst also allowing me to strategically work to my brand strengths. Warren provides a wealth of personal experiences as a process to attack your digital environment head on. As a modern entrepreneur be inspired to Think Digital first!"

Toyan Greaves, CEO of *Vinyl Vandals.*

AWARD WINNING ENTREPRENEUR AND DIGITAL MARKETING EXPERT SHARES HOW TO BUILD A SOCIALLY-SAVVY BUSINESS

Technology has disrupted many of the traditional ways businesses conduct their sales and marketing strategy meaning the only constant is 'change'. You could call it a technological revolution, one that has changed the business landscape permanently.

In this book, entrepreneurs will be taken on a journey that will ensure they are fully equipped to understand the importance of the world wide web, its purpose in business and how to put together an effective strategy that will provide them with a competitive advantage over those who choose to ignore this exciting new digital landscape.

Websites are no longer a luxury add-on to the marketing mix but a necessary tool that if understood and used effectively with social media and digital marketing, will have a positive effect on a whole business strategy.

Warren guides individuals through the step-by-step process that will help them stay ahead of their competition. By engaging with this book, they will be able to use all the tools, tips and tactics that can build a strong business strategy to help them stay focused on their sales and marketing from a digital perspective.

When you are reading each chapter of **Think #Digital First**, you will be taken on a journey. This journey will cover everything from your personal profile system, day-to-day planner, SWOT analysis, defining your target customer and brand style guide.

As you get further through the book, I will share with you;

- Daily business plan
- 12-month cash flow forecast
- SEO Research template
- Meta-data implementation template
- 90-day go-to-market strategy
- 90-day marketing plan
- 5-day sales process

For you to get the most out your journey through this workbook, I have made all of the above and much more available for you to download from **www.ThinkDigitalFirst.com** and **www.warrenknight.co.uk**

If you wish to stay up-to-date with the latest technology to help your company grow, come and join me on Twitter **@WarrenKnight** and use **#askwk** to share with me your personal experiences and how **Think #Digital First** has helped your business grow and I'll share your success to over 25,000 followers across my social networks.

I also run complimentary monthly "educational" webinars where I co-host with industry experts so that they can share their knowledge with you. To find out more, sign-up to my monthly newsletter today at **www.warrenknight.co.uk**.

Your journey doesn't stop after reading **Think #Digital First**. I have built an engaging community over the last 7 years and I hope that after reading this book, you will also take that next step and utilise my past and future webinars, workshops and advice to grow your business.

DEDICATED TO

This dedication goes out to the people that consciously and sub-consciously have been close to me throughout this book production process; helping me to bring a life-long dream to reality.

My youngest sister, Starr you are truly amazing and have been a constant support during the past five years (even though I fired you twice). You have been there during the highs and lows and always surprised me with your strength and knowledge, despite being just 24 years old.

Mum, you know I love you so much. Your energy, your lust for life and how you get every ounce of joy from every moment. I hope I can love life as much as you at your age.

Lloyd, Karl, Patrice, Scott, Vinni, Stevie, Tarquin, I have known you all for more than 20 years and I know sometimes I might not say it enough; "I love you guys".

My team, you have all helped me take my vision and turn it into a book I am proud of. Dimitria, your attention to detail and passion is infectious; Rob you have delivered an amazing website. Vicky and Spencer, your creativity and visual foresight, to take my branding across multiple platforms, giving me brand consistency. Wendy, Lisa and not forgetting Chris, you have all played your part, thank you.

To all the people I've met during the past 25 years that have made me smile, brought me to tears, challenged me and held my hand through my darkest moments. You know who you are and I thank you all.

Lastly, to you Paris, even though we are very different people, I love you and will always be here for you.

"In this book, I am going to take you through the Seven Simple Steps that took 25 years in the making. If you follow each step with me, you will have the knowledge to grow your business from the ground up. Think #Digital First and let's turn your passion into a socially-savvy business."

WARREN KNIGHT

THINK
#DIGITAL
FIRST

7 SIMPLE STEPS
to a
SOCIALLY SAVVY BUSINESS

TECHNOLOGY | SALES | MARKETING

Filament
Publishing

Published by
Filament Publishing Ltd
16, Croydon Road, Waddon, Croydon,
Surrey, CRO 4PA, United Kingdom
Telephone +44 (0)20 8688 2598
Fax +44 (0)20 7183 7186
info@filamentpublishing.com
www.filamentpublishing.com

ISBN - 978-1-910125-98-4

Printed by: 4edge Limited

CONTENTS

FOREWORD

With more than 1 billion people now online, and increasingly looking for British made products and services, it's become essential for Britain's small businesses to embrace the web and go digital.

The cost to get online is low and yet the benefits run deep. With template website builders, you can have a home on the web for less than £50 and then, leveraging social media, attract people from across the world to visit that website to browse or buy.

Tools such as Twitter, Pinterest, Facebook and LinkedIn have enabled the small business owner to look and think big and to do so on a budget.

What's required to make the most of this digital opportunity is awareness of the available tools, a commitment to keeping up to date with what's new and coming online, and an openness to seek advice from digital experts.

One of those experts is Warren Knight and in this helpful book he sets out the key things you need to know to think digital and grow your business.

Warren starts with advice that 'working on yourself is just as important as building your business' and goes on to offer tips, tools and techniques to understand your customers, engage with them across the web, network with confidence, create actionable plans and how to make the most of your working day!

His knowledge is based on years of experience of supporting entrepreneurs.

It's a must read book to help you on your digital way.

Emma Jones – MBE founder of Enterprise Nation

"This book will take you through the process of helping you to embrace technology, to Think #Digital First and focus on sales and marketing for your business."

WARREN KNIGHT

INTRODUCTION

25 YEARS IN THE MAKING

HIP HOP DANCER TO ENTREPRENEUR AND AUTHOR

First of all, I'd like to share my story with you, to show you where I have come from.

It's 1983 and it's a Saturday. Today is the day I get my pocket money. I'm making so much noise in the kitchen, willing to wake up my Dad . I can hear his footsteps leaving the bedroom and approaching the top of the stairs. As he walks down the stairs, I run from the kitchen to meet him and, with a smile on his face, he gives me £1 pocket money. I open the garage door, grab my "flame red" Rally Grifter and cycle to our local village. Living in a little village called Studham (next to Whipsnade Zoo) in Bedfordshire, it takes about 10 minutes to pedal as fast as my little legs could take me. Going past my friends' houses, the local garage and into the village past the Red Lion, owned by the parents of my first crush Phoebe, I finally make my way to the world's best sweet shop (in my opinion) Maisy's.

I get off my bike, lean it against the glass window and walk through the door where a little bell chimes and alerts Maisy's attention. She looks up and says "Good morning Warren" to which I reply in a high-pitched voice (as my voice had not broken yet) "Morning Maisy". "Would you like the usual Warren?" Maisy says and of course, my usual was none other than cola cubes. She twists the blue lid off, picks up a little yellow scooper and scoops a 1/4 worth of cola cubes and places them into a little white bag. Twisting the bag around and around so it's closed, she hands the bag to me with a big smile on her face. I give her my £1 from my Dad, get my change and leave the shop.

I get back on my bike and cycle home as fast as my little legs would take me, hoping one of my friends, Chris, Kevin or Nigel would be outside playing, so I could share with them the journey I'd just been on and offer them a cola cube (if they were lucky).

Fast forward - to being a little bit older, a little bit wiser and with a few extra grey hairs.

I live in London and its Sunday. I go down to my local farmers market and collect my weekly organic food. I walk to my favourite fish stall where the owner, Chris says "Morning Warren", I respond in my now broken voice "Morning Chris". Chris asks if I want my usual to which I reply "No thanks, I'd like the salmon today please Chris". He leans over the counter to pick up the salmon and I ask him to hold on a second. Why; to take a picture? I pull out my iPhone, open up my Instagram App take a picture of the salmon, checking into the location using Foursquare (or Swarm as it's now known) and share the image across four different social networks to more than 20,000 people, in a split second.

The reason I have shared this story with you is to highlight how the world has evolved with the use of technology; even though our natural human instinct has not.

This book will take you through the process of helping you to embrace technology, to **Think #Digital First** and focus on sales and marketing for your business.

Entrepreneurship was in my blood from a young age. I used to make chocolates at night with my Mum, using shell shapes and take them to school, to sell for extra pocket money. This was when business became a passion for me.

In 1983, my passion became a lot more realistic and looking back now, I can see that this is when I started to pave my career as a business owner. I was listening to Capital Radio, where Tim Westwood was playing his usual Hip Hop Show booming from my Bush double tape deck stereo. A year later, the film "Breakdance" was released and from that moment, I was hooked on learning how to lock, pop, break and do the "turtle". Not, and I repeat, not, the twerk.

I passed my driving test at 17 and borrowed my Dad's car so I could drive with my friends to London, more specifically to Camden Palace (now Koko's) to bust-a-move. This made me realise my passion for all types of music from Jazz and Hip-Hop to Funk and Soul.

"PROFESSIONAL
hip hop
DANCER"

Fast forward to 1989, with fashionably long hair; when illegal raves were sprawled across the national newspapers and TV was talking about the new phenomenon of kids partying in fields till sunrise, with DJs spinning tunes all night. I loved to dance and I soon realised I could make a profession out of entertaining people. When I was spotted and asked to dance on stage for a fee, I was delighted and surprised. How amazing to be paid £100s to do what I love and at that moment, I knew I had to make a move and go with this new opportunity. At the age of 20, I moved to London and immersed myself in the music scene. I auditioned for a TV show called Dance Energy, hosted by Normskie. A week later, I was on live TV in front of millions of people, doing what I loved; dancing professionally.

In 1991, when the World Wide Web (www) was launched, I spotted a niche in the clubbing scene and used the web to launch the first drum and base club. I set this up during the day on a Sunday, at The Gardening Club, in Covent Garden. The venue was perfect for giving clubbers the feeling of still being night time. Soon I expanded and hired venues, including: The Old Limelights; and Kensington High Street; mixing house music with drum and bass for special day/night events during Bank Holidays and New Year's Eve. As amazing as it was to be out partying all night and sleeping during the day, I soon realised that I wanted a real business. One, where I could wake up on a Monday morning, with a coffee and go to my office, dial up to the internet via a modem and start working.

It's 1992, the 1st birthday of the www and with very little money I wanted to start a business. I needed help from people that knew how to set up and run a business. So I approached The Prince's Youth Business Trust. I was offered business training, help preparing my first business plan and six months later, a loan of £5,000. My first real commercial business Melodic Distribution was born. It was a clothing and music (12" record and mix tapes) partnership company which started distributing industry-recognised brands such as, Ministry of Sound, Strictly Rhythm and Dee Jay Recordings. I started doing trade shows in the UK and Europe, selling nationally as well as internationally.

" IN 1991 THE WWW
was
LAUNCHED "

My business partner at the time Chakan and I quickly realised that a business cannot survive on 15% commission, so we opened a stall in Camden to sell direct to consumers. This was at a time in the 90s when eCommerce barely existed for small businesses. However, we very quickly understood that what the customer needed and wanted was guiding us as to what to buy.

After a couple of great years, we realised that we wanted to go in different directions and embark on our own separate, business careers. In 1995, I stepped down as Director and set up my own "State of the Art" clothing range selling skateboard/snowboard t-shirts, sweats, hoodies and bags. After sponsoring the UK No.1 skateboarder at the time, my business grew very quickly. I discovered that my ex-partner had closed down Melodic Distribution, which left a gap in the market. So I decided to partner up with the only company that was recording events up and down the country. Mark converted them into mix tapes and distributing them. This is where Two Tribes (yes, even back in the 90s I was thinking about building tribes) was born. Mark and I set up a warehouse in Watford where we could record, hold stock and offer a pop-in service to buy direct stock. Mark and I worked very hard, we loved what we did, but we put all our time and effort into our business.

By the start of 1997, when eBay was a year old, I was burnt out. I had lost focus and started to feel depressed, under pressure from a health and relationship aspect and I closed down Two Tribes. The next few months were difficult. I stayed at home feeling sorry for myself. I didn't exercise or eat. I'll never forget one cold autumn evening when my partner had come home and had had enough of my negativity. She walked through the door and said, "I never know what mood you're going to be in when I come home and it makes me nervous every time I put the key in the door and wonder what I'm going to walk into".

That was a major turning point for me; and it made me realise that if I didn't do something about the way I was feeling, no one could do it for me.

The next day I walked into our local shop, brought the paper and started searching for sales jobs because I knew sales was one thing I was good at. Going through the classified ads, I saw a small advert looking for salespeople to cover London and various other local counties. Being from Bedfordshire and going to school in Hertfordshire, I felt qualified to go for an interview. I called the number on the advertisement and was asked to come in that afternoon for an interview. I got the job. Even though it was commission only, I had a purpose again. I had a purpose to get up in the morning and to start believing in myself again.

Two weeks into the job, I went into a local London business to discuss how I could help them save money. The meeting went on longer that I planned and little did I know that the owner of the business saw something he liked in me and he asked how I had got the job. It was close to lunchtime and he invited me to lunch at a local Italian restaurant, where he asked me lots of questions about my past. Unbeknown to me, he was interviewing me for a sales role in a company that produced goods in China and sold in the UK and Europe.

He offered me the job and two weeks later I was in Birmingham visiting the Autumn Fair Trade Show and meeting the other members of the staff, with a view to starting work with them a week later. Someone had seen the potential in me and to this day, I have never forgotten that moment. This experience taught me to look past the now, to dig deeper into the past and think about the future when meeting someone for the first time.

In 2000, three years later, when Napster, the file sharing software had celebrated its 1st birthday, I was the Sales Director of Twinklers and managing a team of global sales people with a company turning over millions of pounds. During that time, we designed a unique product that was sold to Children In Need and produced for ASDA. The product was spotted by a Disney representative in Hong Kong and because we had the patent, we were offered a license to produce all of the future Disney characters. In the space of three years, we went from a seven-figure turnover to an eight-figure turnover company. I personally sold into 30 countries from Russia to USA and to South America, utilising the UK Trade and Investment service called OMIS (Overseas Market Introduction Service).

I visited our factory in China three or four times a year and I was travelling for a minimum of 10 days a month to see potential clients and to attend different trade shows in different countries nearly every month. At one stage, I remember being on a plane, getting a taxi to the hotel and going from the hotel to the Expo and back again. I was in a kind of love/hate relationship with travelling and hotels.

During my time travelling, I bumped into an old friend from my Hip Hop and clubbing days who was in my industry. Karl was focused on personal development and invited me to learn more about it. I embraced it with open arms and before I knew it, I had a new zest for life. I started building my knowledge, learning more and more and meeting some amazing people, with amazing stories and I became part of a Mastermind Group. We met up once a month helping each other to become better people, solving problems and making introductions to move forward in our personal or professional careers.

In 2006, Twitter was launched and my whole life changed in a single phone call. A member of my family was not well and was getting worse, actually fatal. I went to the doctors meeting at the hospital with the rest of my family and the news was worse than I had expected.

For the last nine years, I had been so consumed with myself and my life, that I'd forgotten about the people I loved the most. Yes, looking back I was being supportive in the only way I thought I knew how. I had my own problems to deal with and was blinkered to what was happening - right under my nose.

At that moment of realisation, I said to myself, if I can achieve $1 million dollars a month in sales I can do anything. So I gave up work and I did everything I could to help turn this horrible situation into something more positive.

During the next eight months, I had to speak in public for the first time. This was in front of 1,000 people about a fund-raising campaign to pay for medical costs. There was a team of us who appeared on national TV, the front pages of national newspapers, TV talk shows and radio talk shows. We were running events from nightclubs, holding celebrity auctions and much, much more. I'd never been on a journey of so many highs and lows. At one very low point, I remember feeling totally broken and having the realisation that whatever we were doing was not going to change the outcome. That feeling became a reality and the life we were fighting for, ended very suddenly.

I spent the next few months wondering what all the effort was for, and why we could not change what was destined to happen. One significant moment was when I received a phone call from the founder of a charity we had been working with throughout our campaign. It was a charity fighting to save the life of the founder's son, but ultimately, he lost his battle at the age of 21.

At the funeral, he pulled me to one side and said "Two people that come forward during our campaign and donated blood, had saved the lives of two other children." I burst into tears, because it made me realise that it's not always about the destination, but rather the journey that we go on. Life is full of surprises.

I went back to work for the same firm and after 12 months of getting over our family loss; I decided to focus on one magical moment from the campaign. It was when one of the premiership footballers, Jermain Defoe who we had been working very closely with, spoke about our campaign on Facebook and promoted our website. During the next 24 hours, we had more hits to the website than we'd ever seen in one day. Offers of help both in time and money came rolling in. I realised in that day how powerfully an influencer in a social network can engage with their audience and get them to take action. Yes, it was an emotional ask but nevertheless the results spoke for themselves. So I decided I'd had enough of working with Disney and selling into corporates like ASDA, Sainsbury's, New Look, M&S and international retailers. It was time for a change.

DropBox was launched in 2008, which I love and speak about later on in this book. It was also the first year I really understood the power of the internet. How it can help companies reach their target audience without having to travel around the world, nor set up trade shows at an extortionate cost without ever knowing if you will receive a ROI (return on investment).

After researching the best Internet Marketers globally, I discovered that America was leading the world. At that time, a few UK organisations were inviting these American experts to share their knowledge with small groups of people, for a cost, in the hope of applying their learning to their businesses.

I was fascinated by what I saw going on and I decided to write a book about it, in fact I decided to write three books, as I have never really done things by half. The first book was a sales book about how I achieved $1million sales in one month and what the strategy was behind that process.

" $1 MILLION SALES
in
ONE MONTH ,,

The second book explained how a UK based business could sell and grow internationally by setting up offices, distributors and partners in various countries. With the experience I had gathered during my

Disney days, I felt I had the knowledge to give to others and I put this first-hand experience into my first business books.

The third book was about social media for business. I had spent the best part of a year understanding this new landscape and I wanted to let companies know how they could use it to build their brand, locally, and internationally.

I felt ready to help companies understand social media to achieve brand growth and increase sales. I decided to return to the trade shows that I once disliked so much; this time not as an exhibitor, but as a speaker. I knew if I could speak to a room full of people in my industry who were there to listen and learn; I could turn my years of knowledge into a useful journey for them and a business for me.

I found an amazing designer, called Gary who developed my first Warren Knight brand and built me a website that reflected my knowledge and showed how I could help companies to grow. I have always done things that I am passionate about, but at this point on my career journey, I felt I had found something I truly loved and was good at, which also added value to other people; public speaking.

However, being good was not good enough for me, as although changing industry and business models was not easy, encouraging companies to embrace the power of the internet and digital marketing was a hard task. After several personal setbacks, including getting divorced and giving up work for eight months, I was not in a good financial situation and I started to feel frustrated. I knew, however I needed help.

The help I needed came in the form of a mentor. Someone who had been very successful in their life, against many odds; I had the upmost respect for Paul and so I asked him to be my mentor. After coming to watch me speak at an event, we sat in his car for nearly two hours talking. Everything he said about me was true and it brought me to tears, although, I knew he was the right person to help me go to the next stage in my professional and personal life.

For the next three months, I had the most intense emotional roller coaster of a ride, learning to truly understand myself and what was important to me. I had to do this so that I could define my next journey. Also, I learnt to understand other people better and because of this, I became a better speaker.

During this time, I had the help of two very different coaches. One, Mac an internationally renowned professional speaker whose style is very structured, but personal and that was what I needed for my talks. The other, Steve a comedian and also a professional speaker. With this professional help, I finally found the real me and I learnt how to bring my personality onto the stage, in a structured way. In fact, I actually found the perfect combination for my personality type.

By 2010, the birth of Instagram, which sold for $1 billion to Facebook, I was speaking at more and more events and trade shows and to hundreds of companies, learning about their business growth problems.

I began to realise there was a massive gap in the eCommerce market for companies wanting to sell online. At this time, there was no self-service, online store builder that was simple and easy to use and offered a big brand experience such as ASOS or John Lewis.

I called a friend of mine Syd who had helped me out with our fund-raising campaign in 2007 and together we discussed the issues that UK brands were facing. Also, I conducted marketplace research and discovered there was nothing available that matched what I was talking about. Nothing that incorporated the big brand experience with the features and functionality of a big brand; but utilising the power of social media and digital marketing to grow businesses online. My friend loved the idea but was not in a position to help me financially. He was a shareholder of a small creative digital agency and suggested I speak to the founders, which I did.

A few weeks later, we'd come up with a new brand, a business model and a route to market. During the next few months his team of developers built the UK's 1st social sharing eCommerce platform, designed to give SMEs a big brand experience offering a multi-channel experience and Gloople was launched.

GLOOPLE

gloople.

In 2011, Google took a second stab at building a social network to compete with Twitter and Facebook, this became Google+. This was when Gloople (the name came from the desire to "glue" "people" together) launched and grew very quickly, turning over six-figures in less than 12 months. We started building eCommerce websites for more brands and we were winning various awards and many accolades in the industry.

By early 2012, we knew the only way to take the company to the next stage was to attract investment. I engaged with an expert in the industry to help us write a business plan and we prepared a three-year cash flow forecast. Three months later, we were ready to go to market. I presented our proposition to a room full of investors and before I had even finished my presentation an investor walked up to me with his business card and said "I want to be your lead investor".

Six weeks later, on the 27th September 2012, the funds were in our bank account, valuing the business at just under £1 million in less than 2 years. To help the investors protect their investment, we were approved for the SEIS (Seed Enterprise Investment Scheme). I highly recommend any business owner to use this scheme if you are less than two years old.

We now had the funds to grow the team and build a SaaS (subscription as a service) platform enabling brands to build their own online store. Two months later, my technology business partner Julian became very ill and he was not able to help the team build a product to revolutionise the online web store space. This caused many concerns for the current shareholders and our investors, so I went back out to the market to find the next round of investment. I also turned to an old friend Tarquin, who I had known for more than 20 years, to either help and or get involved. I needed to stay focused on sales, continue running a technology team, while working with the board members and shareholders. I also needed to prepare a new business plan, with a four-year cash flow forecast and a seven-figure investment.

2013, was about to become one of the most challenging business years I'd ever experienced and after months and months of preparation, finding investors and approaching new challenges head on, we had run out of cash. In September 2013, we had to close the company down. You can image how I felt after three and half years, I had to walk away from our Shoreditch office and start all over again.

I quickly realised that for every positive and negative thing that had happened to me professionally during the past 25 years, the one thing that I always learnt was to grow from every situation and stay true to me.

During the last year, while still maintaining my online profile and looking for ways to add value through education, I saw another need in the market and I helped co-found an online eLearning platform, that's run by a team of virtual staff and does not need an office. We did however receive a loan to help with the marketing from Startup Loans, another great initiative from the UK Government.

This brings me nicely to 2015, and where I am now helping companies to grow, utilising two amazing Government initiatives, providing money to grow the UK economy through SMEs.

1. **Start Up Loans;** I have partnered with Start Up Loans to deliver workshops up and down the country to entrepreneurs taking part in the programme. It's a government-funded scheme to provide advice, business loans and mentoring to startup businesses.

2. **GrowthAccelerator (now part of Business Growth Service);** I am an approved "Growth Coach" delivering Business Development, Access to Finance and Leadership and Management training. I have helped dozens of business owners achieve more than 500% increase in sales. This is the biggest of the initiatives with £200 million grants to give eligible to SMEs.

Both of these are designed for Start Ups to a £40 million turnover (or 250 staff) - companies which want to flourish in the UK.

GROWTHACCELERATOR

BUSINESS GROWTH SERVICE

In this book, I am going to take you through the Seven Simple Steps that took 25 years in the making. If you follow each step with me, you will have the knowledge to grow your business from the ground up. **Think #Digital First** and let's turn your passion into a socially-savvy business.

YOU: THERE WILL ONLY EVER BE ONE

#EXPRESSYOURSELF

"ARE YOU READY?
Probably not
BUT IT'S NEVER TOO LATE TO CHANGE"

An entrepreneur's first step to building a socially-savvy business is accepting that you are the one driving your business forward. To do this in the most successful way, you need to build a social business from the ground up.

It's all about understanding how brands must learn to **Think #Digital First**. This book has been designed to help you embrace the digital technology available and allow you to strategically focus on the two most important aspects of growing a business; sales and marketing.

The lines have been blurred between sales and marketing because of the way businesses and consumers are using the World Wide Web. As an entrepreneur, it is your role to understand all of the aspects of running a business. You need to focus on where your passion and strengths lie and where your weaknesses are and build a strong team around you.

What makes a successful entrepreneur?

Here are 10 traits of successful entrepreneurs. You might already have these or you might be developing them. They are important to understand and take on board, to make sure that the reason your business is successful, is because of you.

1. Take time out for yourself

2. Do what you love

3. Take what you do seriously

4. Invest in yourself

5. Become an expert in your field

6. Be a plan-a-holic

7. Be open to change

8. Manage your money wisely

9. Stay up to date with technology

10. Understand your strengths and weaknesses

The reason it is critical to mention these 10 traits at the beginning is because to be a successful you and #expressyourself - is to inspire you, to be a better version of yourself. There are a number of people I have encountered in my professional and personal life that inspire me every single day with their words and advice. Without having people around me that have my best interests at heart and always challenge me to improve myself, I would never had the strength to write this book.

Stop what you are doing and think

Realign yourself. Look ahead. Where are you going in the next chapter of your life? It wasn't until I was sat in that car with my friend and business mentor that I really stopped to question myself. In that moment, I allowed my barriers to come down and to be okay with feeling vulnerable. It was a positive experience and gave me the refocus I needed, to see what was important to me. To coin the phrase "intelligence high, emotions low", I had to commit and make intelligent decisions.

What am I doing wrong?

You could be reading this book because of the overwhelming feeling of not knowing which way to turn. Have you asked yourself; Why do these things keep happening to me? I know I have.

There is such a thing as a vicious circle and it's difficult to find a way out of the loop of negative actions once you are bound up in them. There are habits in life that we keep repeating; even knowing they are not good for our personality. Take baby steps when changing the direction of your life and build a better, happier and healthier you.

I'm sure you've heard the saying that we have two of these (ears) and one of those (mouth). In other words spend more time listening.

" TWO EARS FOR LISTENING —— *and* —— ONE MOUTH FOR SPEAKING ,,

Question yourself?

What is it that is causing you to have this blockage that's stopping you from moving forward? Is it time? Money? Family? Location? Give each of these a rating on a scale of 1 to 10. Look at your results and find the pain point, the highest score that hurts the most. Work out for yourself or with a mentor or business coach, where you have to put in the time to sort out these issues.

A great starting point is asking yourself; What's important to me?

It might be going to the gym, green juicing, or going to the cinema once a week. Whatever it is, start with the simple things in life and decide what your daily/weekly/monthly personal expectations are in all areas of your life.

What do you love?

Your Mum? Dog? Car? New trainers? Whatever it is, reconnect to the inner you, build new habits and chose to make a decision with a positive mind set.

Figure out where you are now

What does that look like? Are you genuinely happy with how your life is going for you and if not, how do you get to where you want to go? Self-belief is a strong push for any entrepreneur. Once you believe in what you can achieve, you can face any situation head on and build your future exactly the way you want it to be.

I started to write this book more than 12 months ago, but I was not in the right place, not physically, nor emotionally and spiritually. Every step I took was like swimming upstream. Once I realised this, I stopped pushing against the tide, took a step back and put the book down for a while, leaving it alone until I was fully ready to pick it up again and complete it.

Mapping out the process and a timeline for yourself is a fantastic way to help you know if you have the time and commitment to complete the task. Also, having a dedicated timeline keeps you accountable throughout this process.

It's time to invest in you!

Throughout my life, I've found better people than me to learn from. One of the most important things you need to remember as an entrepreneur and business owner is to take massive action in your learnings and apply it to the specific areas of your personal or business life that you want to develop and grow.

Find your own voice

Yes it's ok to model yourself on your peers but make it your own style and always do everything with honesty and integrity. Be around positive people and stay away from negative energy. Develop your awareness of negative energy so you can see it clearly and know when it's around you and stopping you from doing what you want to do.

What is it that I do right?

Have you ever been in a relationship where after a few years, you both start to grow in different directions? One way of dealing with this is to write down together the areas where each person feels the other person has changed. You can do the same for yourself.

When you want to get the best results out of what you are doing, you need to focus on the things you like and the things you know you're good at. This gives your mind the power to compare and add contrast to all the options you have to move forward. Knowing and using what you are good at, is empowering. Using strategies that have worked for you before is taking positive action to achieve what you want.

Get rid of fear and take control of you

To give you an example; the one thing that has stayed constant during the last 25 years is me and I have never stopped learning or growing. When I was only 20 years old, I experienced the power of this. I was on stage at a big event, in front of a huge crowd dancing for Shades of Rhythm. I remember misjudging the stage and falling straight into the crowd. I can assure you this never happened again. While I have made many mistakes (some big, some small) I've always learnt from them to become a better person, both in my personal life and in business.

At each stage of your journey, you must always be making notes and evaluating the process, ultimately paying attention to every action, and reaction and systemising. If you are not ready to break the old habits and build new ones, then pause and take some time away from the immediate issue and come back to it later.

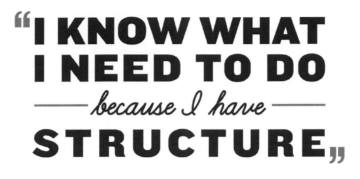

"I KNOW WHAT I NEED TO DO
— because I have —
STRUCTURE,,

I have a process in place for everything I do, including building my team to help me visualise, design, write and deliver this book for you. Working on yourself is just as important as building your business. There are a number of important factors you need to consider to make your business a success.

Someone who I admire from a personal and business standpoint is Anthony Robbins. He talks about the six Human Needs, which I outline for you below.

1. Certainty/Comfort
With great certainty, comes great comfort. We know there is nothing which is of absolute certainty but the things we value like water flowing from a tap, or our car starting, is one of our important human needs.

2. Variety
Certainty is something which we all desire in life and so is variety. We need to have just enough uncertainty in our lives to give us the variety needed to make our lives more adventurous.

3. Significance
We all want our lives to be important. One of our human needs, is knowing that when we die, our life had meaning and we had been significant enough to help others achieve their goals.

4. Connection/Love
The need for love in humans is overwhelming and building lifelong connections is just as important. We all care and want to be cared for in return.

5. Growth

Growing is a huge part of what every human being wants and needs. To become a better person, increase your knowledge and help others to go through the process of growing.

6. Contribution

Just like significance, we want to feel as if we have contributed to helping others and making the world a better place.

To achieve all of these six human needs, you need to evaluate your personal motivations and see which are the most significant for you. Understanding how you fulfil the needs of others will ultimately make a huge difference in how you do what you do.

When defining your personal journey to improving yourself, the best way to make the biggest improvement, is to KISS it; Keep It Simple Stupid. Taking baby steps on your journey combined with your passion, is a sure fire way to improve your personal growth.

TWO

FRAMEWORK FOR SUCCESS

#THECHOICEISYOURS

Let me ask you a question. Where do you and your business want to be in three years? Or more importantly; where do you see your role in your business in the next 12 months?

Building a framework for success will need to include the key areas around your business. You must know what these are, so you can build the structure of your business on strong foundations.

Sending a random tweet or uploading a photo once a month to Facebook is not enough social media activity for a successful business. For every action or no action there is a reaction. You must always ask yourself: what is the outcome I am seeking to get the result I am looking for?

" SOCIAL MEDIA
—— will not fix a ——
BROKEN BUSINESS „

Online marketing has evolved because of the way businesses have developed during the last five years and to run a socially-savvy and successful business you need to have a complete framework set up from the start to the finish. This will include every part of your business marketing strategy; meaning the old school marketing (picking up the phone or a face-to-face meeting); and new school marketing (tweets, blogs and infographics) to connect with your potential customers. Once you have your customers' attention, you can use an autoresponder to give them something more, such as your latest catalogue or a report that shows the current industry news and you can do this as a digital download, to make it easier for them. Their name and email automatically go into your email marketing campaign system and you can continue to deliver your marketing message to them; adding value, educating and ultimately getting them to buy what you are selling via your online marketing.

This digital process to acquire new customers sounds amazing doesn't it?

However, as it is almost impossible to include every aspect of becoming a socially-savvy business, this book breaks it down for you into meaningful bite size chunks. You now have the right mind set to move forward through this book and this chapter looks at the framework needed for a successful business.

Here is a list of things that you must have the answers for, before you do anything else:

1. What's your business Vision?
2. What's your company's Mission Statement
3. What problem (or pain) does your business solve?
4. What's your USP?
5. What does your target customer look like and what are your markets?
6. Have you done your SWOT analysis?
7. Have you done your branding?
8. What do you charge your customers?
9. What do you do best?
10. What type of staff will you need?

The first step (even if you have been in business for some years) is to design a simple two-page mini business plan. Trust me, it's not as scary as it seems and it doesn't have to be as complicated as you expect #TheChoiceIsYours.

Realigning your business is an intelligent thing to do, so you truly understand where and how your business is going to grow. It doesn't make any difference if you are a startup business or have been trading for three years. Writing a business plan helps you clarify where you are now and where you want to take the business.

To help you build your two-page plan, let's elaborate on these points. This will define the next step you take to grow your business intelligently.

1. Mission Statement defined

A Mission Statement defines what a business does, who its customers are and how it creates value for its customers. A Mission Statement gives you that clarity and focus. Here are two examples.

"To provide our customers with safe, good value, point-to-point air services. To effect and to offer a consistent and reliable product and fares appealing to leisure and business markets on a range of European routes. To achieve this we will develop our people and establish lasting relationships with our suppliers." EasyJet

'To organise the world's information and make it universally accessible and useful'. Google

2. Vision Statement defined

A Vision Statement is a prediction of where the business will be in the future. This can be an emotional driver for those in the company and can be a powerful and purposeful driving force to success. Here are two examples.

"Bringing to the world a portfolio of beverage brands that anticipate and satisfy people, desires and needs." Coca-Cola

"A personal computer in every home running Microsoft software." Microsoft

3. What is the customer's pain you are trying to solve with your product or service?

Knowing this is crucial so you can develop your product and know who you need to be targeting. As a professional speaker, I have come across many small business owners with the same frustration around using social media. What I learnt was that as most small business owners are time short, they want to improve their knowledge from the comfort of their own home. This was the customer problem, which I identified and set out to solve when I co-founded an eLearning platform.

If you know the customers' pain you are trying to solve, you can find the solution. Both the customer problem and the solution need to be congruent with your business goals.

4. USP

" WHAT DOES YOUR USP
— *tell you about your* —
BUSINESS AND TARGET MARKET? "

What is your unique selling proposition? When I was defining the USP for my eCommerce platform, I had to create an elevator pitch, which you can see below.

"The UK's first social sharing eCommerce platform designed for SMEs to have a big brand experience".

Let's break this down, so it is clear.

- The target market at that time and for the 12 months was the UK;

- The unique functionality of the platform was the social sharing aspect and it was the first eCommerce platform to have a social media selling feature, which allowed me to use the word first;

- It was an eCommerce platform (does what it says on the tin);

- The target market were SMEs (small to medium sized enterprises); and lastly

- Focus on the benefit, which for us was the ability to give the customer the same experience they would have on a big brand website, such as BooHoo or Asos.

This is what made us different to our competitors and you need to spend time figuring out what makes your business unique. Defining your USP takes time; I suggest a night in with your friends, pizzas and beers to help challenge you to get the focused and creative answers you need.

To really understand your USP and whether your business has the potential to be successful in the market, you need to do your due diligence. This will include everything from competitor, industry sector and target market research to solving your customers' pain point. Research is an integral part throughout this book demonstrating how completely necessary it is to build strong foundations for a successful, socially-savvy business.

Once your USP has been defined, you can look at your business and decide how you are going to share this with your audience. One question I always ask my clients is. "If you got into a lift with Richard Branson and you only had 30 seconds to describe your business to him, what would your elevator pitch be? Memorising your elevator pitch so you are saying it in your sleep will always guarantee that in the most opportune moments, you can share what your business does with certainty and clarity in just 30 seconds.

5. Target Market
A target market is a group of customers which a business has decided to aim its marketing efforts towards and ultimately its product or service. A well-defined target market is the first element to a marketing strategy and is a critical element to your business strategy so you know that your time, energy and money are being directed in the right direction for your business success.

Deciding on your target market may not be as easy as it seems. It will be time consuming and will take more than just your own input. Firstly, you need to create what I like to call a Wish List.

Wish List

A Wish List is as simple as specifically defining who is going to buy your product or service. You need to identify your target customer by location, interest, age, gender, income, occupation and marital status. You must recognise that you can't do business with everyone and creating your own niche target market will allow you to develop your business in the best possible way.

Valuing each different type of customer and making sure your message reflects this is key to your successful sales and marketing. This is the Value Proposition you are giving your different types of customer and in Chapter Six I'll be explaining what I mean in more detail.

Being laser-focused on your target market is crucial for your business. Once you define who is going to buy your product or service, you know who is most likely going to need your business and the problem you want to solve. Being a big fish in a small pond rather than vice-versa is a more effective strategy for any small business. It is easier to build your reputation and sales if you are more targeted in your marketing.

To fully understand the different types of target customer one really good tip is to give them a name. Until you do that, you only have characteristics that define who you want to target, and once you humanise them by naming them, they become a more realistic business target.

To give you an example, Debbie is my target customer. She is 38 and has two children, lives within the M25 area, has a disposable income, drives an Audi and is time short. Debbie also wants to learn more about social media as she isn't tech-savvy, works full-time and runs her small business on the side. This is my niche target market for one of the technology companies I founded.

Deciding on my target market was not as simple as picking a name and characteristics. You need to look at your own experience, the opportunities around you and your business focus. Think about what you have achieved in the past and what industries you have worked in. This will help you focus on specifically where your knowledge and abilities are, which will give you the guidance you need to find your niche target market.

I named my target customer to create a visual in my mind of who I want to buy my product and once I know this, my marketing strategy becomes easier to design. With an image in your mind and characteristics written down, you can avoid the obvious mistake that "everyone is my target customer".

6. SWOT Analysis

STRENGTHS	WEAKNESSES
These are the skills and services I offer, that others don't.	These are the skills and services others offer, but I don't.
OPPORTUNITIES	THREATS
Here are chances that the market offers, and that I can use for the benefit of my business.	Here are possible market dangers that can threaten the balance and goals of my business.

A SWOT analysis will help you identify the positives and negatives inside your business. You identify, measure and analyse your Strengths, Weaknesses, Opportunities and Threats. Completing a SWOT analysis will help you to:

• improve strategy planning and decision-making;

• determine where change is possible in the business by looking at possibilities and priorities;

• adjust and redefine strategies; and

• explore solutions to your customers' pain.

Remember to look at strengths and weaknesses, opportunities and threats internally and externally. Internal factors include everything from your staff, location, finances and community reputation. External factors include future trends, the economy, business funding, local and national events, as well as changes in demographics and target market as the business grows.

7. Branding

It's easy to look at the big brands such as Nike or Victoria Secret and say yes, that is a successful brand but when it comes to finding your own way as an entrepreneur, branding your business can be challenging. When you develop your branding, you must be authentic, know your values, have your Mission Statement defined and know where you want your business to be in the future.

Building your brand starts with you. Your consumer needs a reason to buy your product or service and that begins with a human connection. Consumers know what they want and your brand must reflect this. To offer your consumers an engaging experience, your branding needs to reflect this visually. It is critical to have a logo that is recognisable, relatable and is consistent with other images. Take a look at your competitors and see how they have branded their business. It is ok to model yourself on the success of the businesses you see every day.

Finding your branding identity does not happen overnight and can be a long, challenging process and you do need to look to the future. Think three years ahead. Will your branding still be relevant to your consumers? As your business goals change, so might your branding; and be aware that consumers are not fond of change. Bear in mind that strong branding will still sell your business in years to come.

Business Image and Direction

What is your ultimate goal? Do you know how you want your business to be perceived online and offline? Do you know where you want your business to be during a long-term period? This book gives you a 90-day Marketing Plan and you also need to be aware of what could potentially happen in the future.

Your brand message can be elaborated on to give more of a vision, culture and stronger customer value. It can be placed across multiple social media and various other online marketing platforms. Keep your branding consistent.

Branding

The branding of your company should portray how you will connect with your target audience. Your logo and other business images should be included in the branding part of your business. Your website must also be branded consistently with your marketing material and your online profiles. Having a brand Style Guide will give conformity to the business and gives new members of your team a single point of reference about the brand and a clear and certain image to identify with.

WK BOOK BRAND GUIDELINES

LOGOS

COLOURS

k100   m100
        y100

CHAPTER NUMBER AND TITLE

ONE

YOU: THERE WILL ONLY EVER BE ONE

#EXPRESSYOURSELF

QUOTE

"**SOCIAL MEDIA**
—— will not fix a ——
BROKEN BUSINESS"

BOOK PAGE HEADERS

THINK #DIGITAL FIRST

FOUR   SETTING UP A SOCIALLY - SAVVY BUSINESS

PAGE NO.

12

FONTS

Proxima Nova
For main body text

KNOCKOUT HTF72 FULLCRUISERWT
For callouts and quotes

KNOCKOUT HTF48 FEATHERWEIGHT
For chapter number, chapter name, page number, page book title, page chapter heading

KNOCKOUT HTF26 JUNIORFLYWEIGHT
For chapter hashtags

Learning Curve Pro
For quotes

SF BUTTACUP LETTERING SHADED
Only to be used in AOP

AOP SWATCH
For chapter pages

8. Cost Based Pricing

When designing the final cost price of your product or service, take into consideration the true cost to acquire a customer. As a service driven business, your conversion rate of acquiring a customer might be 50%. This means you have to go through your customer acquisition process twice before you invoice one of those customers. Let me share with you some things you need to think about when acquiring a customer.

1. The initial email
2. First phone call
3. Follow up email
4. Confirmation email of meeting
5. Time it takes to travel to meeting, have meeting and return from meeting
6. Follow up email and proposal
7. Arranging the next meeting to deliver proposal
8. Time to travel, have meeting and return from meeting
9. Preparation of the agreement
10. Sending of the agreement with invoice
11. Follow up email confirming you have received signed agreement and payment into your account

Product driven business e.g. an online retailer, will have to go through various touch points to build brand awareness and gain trust before securing a sale.

1. Organic Search
2. Generic PPC (pay per click) (Google)
3. Generic PPC (Social)
4. Email
5. Text
6. Facebook Update
7. Blog/Article
8. PR (Press Release)
9. Referral
10. Direct Traffic

Every business has a Customer Acquisition Journey and whichever way you look at it, it will cost you, whether it's time or cash because your time is valuable and has a price. These are some of the actions that either you, or your staff can take before you even deliver on the product or service your business produces. It is important you value your time and you associate a cost to this time. This must be part of your final cost price on delivering that service or product.

9. What Do You Do Best?

When I was looking at building my first technology company, I knew what my strengths were and that my 25 years experience in sales and marketing was where I would excel in the business. What I couldn't provide with my experience, I knew I needed to bring in with outside help. To build a technology product, I needed an accountant, administrator, web developer and designer in my team to move forward. However, this is unique and different for every business.

Really think about where your strengths and weaknesses lie within the business, to help you build the right team around you for the job you need to do, to encourage business growth. If you are finding it hard to define this, a great tool to use is DISC Personality Profiling, which stands for the individual characteristics of: Dominance; Influence; Steadiness; and Conscientiousness. It is a 15-minute assessment which will help you determine your personal profile as well as your strengths and weaknesses.

"Get DISC here for FREE" – www.tonyrobbins.com/ue/disc-profile.php

The assessment gives you a choice of four words, which you rank according to what your preference is, or which answer is most like you or least like you. This is followed by more ranking questions which define your personal strengths and values. At the end you can download your results as a PDF document.

Knowing these results will help you understand who you need to develop to have the best possible team for your business. Once you have done the DISC profile, it is a good idea to have your team do it as well. Be the leader and someone your team looks up to, by encouraging your own personal growth, as well as encouraging theirs. So, why is your team so important?

10. What Type of Staff Do You Need?

It will take great, decisive leadership to build the best team for your business. You will have to make difficult decisions and establish standards of performance that must be met by every team member. Building an effective team means understanding those around you, their strengths and ultimately, what makes them happy in the workplace. It is an art and a science building a team.

Here are three different ways of doing it. Depending on where your business is and the type of business you run, you will find one of these more suitable than the others.

Employee

An employee is someone you hire to work inside your business and give a specific area to focus on.

Virtual Assistant

A virtual assistant (VA) is someone who is self-employed and provides expertise in administration, technology, creativity (social) or sits in an assistant role from the comfort of their own home. This means you are not responsible for their overheads.

Contractor

A contractor is someone who you bring into the business for a short period to focus on a specific task within the business. They will be experts in their field and they cost more but are only there for the short term.

This chapter has included the main areas you need to build the framework for a successful business and to keep your journey moving forward as an entrepreneur. The next chapter will help you manage your time so you can focus on what is important.

Team

This isn't the first time and it definitely won't be the last time I mention how important it is to have the right team around you when building your socially-savvy business. Do you have the right skills to deliver the outcome need for your Marketing Plan? If not, you will need to:

hire an agency; or freelancers; or bringing in someone to do this for you. You will need a Marketing Management Content Plan, including:

- Social Media Marketing;

- Pay Per Click Campaigns;

- Search Engine Optimisation;

- Website Management;

- Writing Articles;

- Image Creation;

- Email Marketing; and

- Content Marketing.

If you don't want to spend an extortionate amount of money hiring people to do this work for you, hire a VA (Virtual Assistant). I have two VAs, one who specialises in business development and one in online marketing.

THREE

PROTECTING YOUR TIME: FOCUS ON SALES

#INSANEINTHEMEMBRANE

"ARE YOU *a* BUSY FOOL?"

As an entrepreneur, you are always going to be busy. The questions is, are you a busy fool? This is an industry term, used to describe someone who is doing a lot of things, but not owning their time or growing their business #InsaneInTheMembrane.

I am passionate about this step in the process of building a social-savvy business because this was where I was in 2008. It wasn't until I began working with my mentor that I really started to build my personal brand and grow my businesses. He shared with me some simple and really effective techniques, which helped me to own my time and stay focused on what I wanted to achieve, and you can do it too.

It is critical to understand where you are spending your time. Here is a document to help you which will inform you of what you should be doing every 30 minutes of your waking day. Using this document will give you clarity and focus and a deeper understanding of where you spend your time.

	Monday	Tuesday	Wednesday	Thursday	Friday
09:00	To do list	Social Media	Social Media	Social Media	Social Media
09:30	Preparation				
10:00	Social Media				
10:30	Social Media				
11:00	Emails				
11:30	Sales Call				
12:00	Sales Call				
12:30	VA Call				
13:00	Lunch				
13:30	Lunch				
14:00	Marketing				
14:30	Marketing				
15:00	Emails				
15:30	Travel				
16:00	Meeting				
16:30	Meeting				
17:00	Travel				
17:30	Debrief				
18:00	Preparation				

ADD YOUR ACTIONS HERE

Did you know that management in businesses wastes six weeks per year looking for lost documents? Time management is something many successful, busy entrepreneurs struggle with. If this is you, I am going to share with you some tips to help you better manage your time. Further on in the book, there are also some tools you can use to protect your time.

When it comes to your working day remember to spend some time planning. . To save time, you will need to spend time and it's ok to do that, especially if it means your days are more organised. Remember the Pareto Principle, which states that 80% of your success will come from 20% of your activity. Work out what that 20% of your activity is that drives your 80% success, so you know to give priority to those activities.

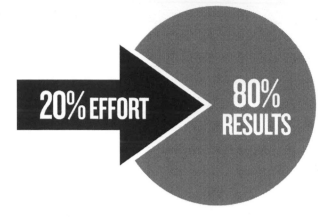

It can be hard to let go and allow others to help you complete tasks but you will need to do this if you have a lot on your plate. Delegate to others in your business the less important tasks and those that are not aligned to your strengths and outsource where possible. Sometimes, things come up that cannot be avoided and it's not the end of the world if this happens. Make sure the most important tasks are completed before anything else so that if you have interruptions, you know your important tasks have been accomplished.

This is a great visual analogy. Imagine three empty glass tubes in front of you; the first is empty; the second has small rocks; and the third has big rocks. How can you get tubes 2 and 3 into tube 1?

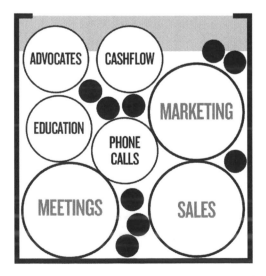

This is where the term "get your big rocks in first" comes from. Once you have all the big rocks in the tube, the small rocks (smaller tasks) can fit around the important tasks (big rocks).

Having deadlines will prevent tasks from dragging on too long. When I know I have a lot to get done in one day, I will always set myself a deadline so I push myself to finalise what needs to be completed. We are not robots we are human beings. Unfortunately, we can't work 24 hours, 7 days a week. Knowing your limits between work and free time is very important too. Without living a balanced life, what was once the work that you enjoyed, becomes a chore.

What is your biggest distraction? A big distraction of mine when I am trying to complete an important task is my mobile phone. It takes 23 minutes to recover from every interruption. I, like many millions in the world, feel uncomfortable being separated from my smartphone. However, I have learned that by removing this distraction I accelerate moving forward with my daily tasks.

Your Prime Time
When are you most focused during your working day? Your prime time is the time when you are the most proactive in completing important tasks. This can be in the morning, around lunchtime or in the evening. Make sure you attend to important tasks during the time you are feeling your best, your highest. Allocating the appropriate time to each of these areas is about breaking old habits and forming new ones.

These tips can help you improve your time management. Give them a go.

We are now going to consider other important areas within your business. Ask yourself how many of the tips below you are doing and if they aren't within your skill set or not a high priority task, are you delegating them to staff members or VAs?

As an entrepreneur we wear lots of different hats. Each of these different hats needs to be a part of your weekly habit. The amount of time you spend on them must be focused and dedicated.

The Different Hats of a Business Owner

The lines between sales and marketing have become blurred because of the way we now communicate online and use digital technology. Therefore, the need for clarity in business is even more important.

Sales

Sales are always the lifeblood and pumping heart of any business. To focus on sales, you must have a very clear Go to Market Strategy. This will share your business USP in the right way, from day one, to the right target audience.

When was the last time you did your due diligence to find your business three new customers?

Or more importantly, when did you upsell or cross sell current customers/clients? An astounding 61% of consumers take their business to a competitor when they end a business relationship. Once you have found your target customers, are you taking them through what is called the Customer Acquisition Journey?

Define what works and what doesn't for your business and your customers.
This is about creating a process for your business to become a well-oiled machine that continuously brings in prospects through your marketing funnel into your sales process.

This is how to do it:

1. Build trust;
2. Engage;
3. Convert; and
4. Build brand advocates.

While I was looking to acquire Channel Partners for my technology company or helping a business owner as a coach, I had to protect my time. This includes understanding how many 30 minute calls you need to make followed by how many one-hour meetings you need to have to acquire one customer. Out of every three phone calls, you might have two meetings, and acquire one customer. If this is true to your business, you know that your ratio is at 3:1 (three phone calls = one customer).

If you're an online store, you need to have a conversation rate of 3%. This means it's all about driving target traffic on a consistent basis. Remember: the more traffic, the more sales.

Determining this will help you understand the value of your time and your true worth. Once you have acquired a customer; what is the lifetime value of this customer? You need to know how much total cost and time you have spent acquiring that customer and working with that customer from the beginning to the end. This will help you calculate your customer's worth and how much your time is worth.

Do you market research your competitors and benchmark their pricing structure against yours? Remember: find your micro-niche and increase your worth.

"FIND YOUR MICRO-NICHE —— *and* —— INCREASE YOUR WORTH"

Marketing

As a modern day entrepreneur, you must **Think #Digital First**. For example, when you are wearing your marketing hat and going to a networking event, do your market research to determine who you want to spend your time with and connect with them online before you arrive through various social networks, (my favourites are Twitter and LinkedIn). This is a great way to open a conversation and start a new business relationship. Start by talking about your passion for helping people and remember you do not need to put yourself into sales mode in the first 30 seconds, because you have already built rapport online.

Some of the best businesses with massive growth in the last 5-10 years are those, which have been creative in their marketing and brand positioning. You can model their success, making it your own, by being transparent and bringing your personality and business vision to your marketing strategy.

Taking on the marketing role in your business means you will have to spend time building relationships offline and online, with your potential and existing customers/clients whether they are direct customers or acquired via a channel partner. Keeping consistent with your brand message and online voice is crucial.

In your marketing, you need to determine an online and offline approach to your 90-day Marketing Plan. Your offline Marketing Plan will include everything from public speaking and trade shows to magazine ads, direct mailings, networking events and even cold calls. I'll talk more about this in Chapter Six.

Finances

Managing your finances can be difficult if you don't have a background in this field of expertise. Having happy customers who are prepared to pay for your product is great. However, if you don't understand your P&L (profit and loss) you won't know where you stand with your business finances. Here is a simple 12-month cash flow forecast for you to plug your numbers into.

Did you know that 80% of paper and information that we keep, we never actually use?

Accountability for cash flow is something every entrepreneur needs to take on board as a responsibility of running a business. Knowing what your burn rate is (monthly expenses - office space, staff costs, travel costs, stationery) gives you the knowledge to focus on bringing in sales to the business to make it profitable. If you don't know what your true costs are in a business, how much time do you know to give yourself to focus on sales?

CASH FLOW FORECAST - 12 MONTHS

Month:	Pre Start	1	2	3	4	5	6	7	8	9	10	11	12	Totals
Receipts														
Cash Sales														£0
Collections from credit sales														£0
New equity inflow														£0
Loans received														£0
Other														£0
Total Receipts	£0	£0	£0	£0	£0	£0	£0	£0	£0	£0	£0	£0	£0	£0
Payments														
Equipment														£0
Payments to suppliers														£0
Staff wages														£0
Rent														£0
Utilities														£0
Insurance														£0
Travel														£0
Telephone														£0
Postage														£0
Office supplies														£0
Advertising														£0
Marketing/promotion														£0
Bank charges														£0
Miscellaneous														£0
Directors' salaries														£0
Loan repayments														£0
Other														£0
Total Payments	£0	£0	£0	£0	£0	£0	£0	£0	£0	£0	£0	£0	£0	£0
Cashflow Surplus/Deficit (-)	£0	£0	£0	£0	£0	£0	£0	£0	£0	£0	£0	£0	£0	£0
Opening Cash Balance	£0	£0	£0	£0	£0	£0	£0	£0	£0	£0	£0	£0		
Closing Cash Balance	£0	£0	£0	£0	£0	£0	£0	£0	£0	£0	£0	£0		

Month:	Pre Start	1
Receipts		
Cash Sales		
Collections from credit sales		
New equity inflow		
Loans received		
Other		
Total Receipts	£0	£0

Operations

How technically-savvy are you?

The world of the internet has now (while it has built millionaires who work from home) lost the fine art of communicating with people and managing people in a way that shows the best of their abilities.

Maintaining a website; daily use of social media and digital marketing; and understanding Google are three important technical aspects of running a business you, or one of your team members need to be experts at. Remember, your time is priceless. Doing something technical that will take you two hours when someone more experienced will only take 20 minutes, is time better spent.

Another part of maintaining your website along with managing the marketing content is through copywriting. If you are responsible for this, you automatically become the copywriter for your business, which is time heavy. Do you have the ability to work at the speed needed for copywriting, as well as the accuracy? Think about this, seriously.

These days, copywriting is integral and the average online content marketing spend should be a minimum of 30% of your overall marketing budget for whatever size business. It should be up to 80% if you are an online business. This is why having a copywriter that understands the tone of your business is the future of business online.

If you want to be responsible for all the copywriting on your website and marketing and sales materials, you will lose a lot of time, which could be better spent elsewhere on the business to bring in the money. I know that copywriting is not my expertise, so I have brought someone into my business who has the particular knowledge needed, at a small cost.

There are some great websites you can use to find experienced freelance copywriters for a reasonable price, if you do not have the experience or confidence to do it yourself. See Chapter Five.

As a business owner, delegation is something that cannot be avoided. The appointment of a responsibility to another team member is how I define delegation. Successful people start with a core skill set like sales. Evolving into an entrepreneur and building a team is about creating the right atmosphere and learning to manage different personalities. The art of delegation comes from being a great manager. Excelling in sales doesn't mean you know how to manage five members of staff.

To work well with your team, you need to understand the strengths and weaknesses of each team member. As the founder of your business, you need to be a team leader who has the ability to divide tasks between your team, so the most qualified people in each expertise area are doing the right work. Clever hiring from day one will have you standing on strong foundations for fast business growth.

Choose what tasks you want to delegate. As I have mentioned, you should be spending your time on the most critical tasks of your business, not ones that can be easily delegated to other team members. If something doesn't interest you, you don't have to do it. Part of building and working with a team is understanding how to work together productively. This also includes online meetings with virtual staff and face-to-face meetings with people who work in your business full or part-time. Their progress is ultimately, your progress and because you are not with them in an office every day, you need to stay up to date with their daily workings.

"DOES EACH STAFF MEMBER
generate
x3 TIMES THEIR SALARY?"

When delegating, you need to give clear instructions. Spend some time doing this with your team so they fully understand the task at hand. The idea is to save you, as the business owner as much time as possible, so if you are spending too much time hand holding, you should pass the task on to someone else. A great online tool I use to keep track of my team and the tasks they are doing is HubStaff. It takes a screen grab every few minutes and it shows how long they have been working and how productive they have been, while at their computer.

You will come across challenges in the workplace every single day and if you have already built a strong teamwork foundation, your working environment can act as a support mechanism for staff members. It is critical to build a team that work well together and support each other.

At one of my start-up companies, we have a 'Stand Up Scrum' (an interactive and incremental agile software development framework for managing product development) once a day. At the start of the working day, I can hear from each member of my team regarding the work they are doing and how they are finding it. We can discuss ideas to move forward and collectively, come to a decision around certain areas of the business we all agree on. Working as a team is crucial to your success, because a happy team is a money making team.

How are you going to work collaboratively with your team? I would suggest using Google Drive for document sharing; Dropbox for storing collaborative information; and Trello for updating, setting tasks and working together as a team. I have used all three of these tools while writing this book and they all feature in Chapter Five.

Finally, setting a deadline; this is crucial for getting a task completed in a timely manner. Your team need guidance and a part of this includes knowing when a project or task needs to be finished. Make sure you are there for your team when delegating, in case they have any questions only you can answer.

Brand Ambassador

The last hat you need to be able to wear, and in my opinion, one of the most important is being a brand ambassador.

Entrepreneurs can sit in their comfort zone hiding behind the business. The one thing that being in business during the last 25 years has taught me is that businesses come and go. Companies reinvent themselves. Stock markets crash. New ways to market your business evolve. The one thing throughout your life that stays constant is you. You are the one that learns and grows from the failures and successes in your personal and business career. As I touched on in Chapter One, you are the most important part of your business and at this stage of your business, if there is no you, there is no business.

You need to have passion and the knowledge for every part of your business. While you may not, for example, be responsible for the technology or financial part of the business, you are responsible for who is and you need to know they are doing their job to the best of their ability.

Taking on this role means you might have to stand up in front of a room of 40+ people and talk passionately and informatively about your business. Can you do this? Being confident enough to speak professionally, lead your team and build relationships, are what makes a great brand ambassador. It may take time to build these qualities. It is time well spent.

Looking at all the hats you need to wear as a business owner: how many of them can you delegate to a member of your team, so you can save your time and focus on bringing in new clients?

A process that works for me, day in day out, is assigning tasks as the first touch point in the process of speaking to a new customer, to my Virtual Assistant. When someone is interested in speaking with me about how I can help their business grow, I will get my VA to pre-qualify and book in a 30 minute discovery call with the potential client. After I have taken this call, I arrange a one hour meeting face-to-face, if I know I can help this individual with their business and at the end of the meeting we determine whether we will work together.

Managing clients and customers can be difficult, especially when you are balancing your time spent with them, while doing everything else you need to do to keep your business growing.

Here are some ways to help you protect your time:

1.   Keep a to-do list;
2.   Always make notes from each client meeting;
3.   Set achievement goals for your time with each client;
4.   Hold the meeting and manage distractions;
5.   Remember not to overwhelm your clients too much; and
6.   Time manage every client meeting.

Time management is an integral part of building a successful business. While some people may find it easier to focus on just one task at a time, I have come across many people in my industry who think they can multitask extremely well. Before we move onto Chapter Four, I want to talk about multitasking and how it can be used effectively for your time management.

The Art of Multitasking
Surprisingly, multitasking does have its benefits. However, there is bad multitasking and good multitasking. For example, when driving, you should not let your mobile phone distract you, while listening to the radio or talking to the passenger in a car, is deemed ok. All of these have the potential to cause a car crash. However, we have adapted to multitasking, which allows us to do two (or maybe more) tasks at once.

Our brains can handle multiple tasks and it is not dangerous to divide our consciousness. The risk only comes into play when our cognitive resources have too much of a demand - known as the cognitive load. This happens when a task is too severe or time consuming and the ability to perform this task and others at the same time will suffer.

Protecting your time can be difficult. However, with the right tactics you can ensure you are being efficient with your time. Being focused on a task with a deadline and multitasking is not an option. The more focused you are, the better job you will do and the quicker you will achieve your goal.

"STAY FOCUSED
—get the task finished—
AND MOVE ON„

One of the best ways to protect your time is to stay away from emails. They can, at times, become a black hole where you lose hours of your precious time. To avoid being sucked in, remember not to look at your emails until you have completed your important tasks. If you are struggling to do this, set a timer so you only spend, say 10 minutes going through emails. Another way to stay time efficient is to keep a checklist of your daily tasks. Doing this, combined with knowing your limits and not multitasking important tasks, will help you focus on sales, while protecting your time.

FOUR

SETTING UP A SOCIALLY-SAVVY BUSINESS

#EVERYDAYPEOPLE

Welcome to the new world of connecting with your consumers online #EveryDayPeople.

Tim Berners-Lee is a British computer scientist who is considered to be the inventor of the internet, after he wrote a proposal in 1989, which led to the introduction of the World Wide Web or www as we know it today. On 5th September 1997, Google.com was registered as a domain by Larry Page and Sergey Brin.

In April 2000, Google became the search engine we have all grown to use on a daily basis and in 14 years, Google has managed to achieve more than any other company in the history of the internet. This brings us to the next part of your business growth journey through the use of Google and SEO (search engine optimisation).

Since 2007, Tim Berners-Lee has been talking about making the www a web of people and not a web of websites and in September 2013, Google took a giant step forward in this same social direction by introducing Hummingbird. Google Hummingbird judges search queries based on context, which allows Google to give a user the full extent of a search. The whole query is taken into account and not just a word or phrase.

Steve Masters wrote, *"The Hummingbird approach should be inspirational to anyone managing and planning content – if you aren't already thinking like Hummingbird, you should be. In a nutshell, think about why people are looking for something, rather than what they are looking for. A content strategy should be designed to answer their needs, not just provide them with facts."*

As if this wasn't enough for Google users, they introduced another search algorithm in September 2014, which prevented low quality sites and pages from ranking well in the search engine results. This new ability designed by Google was for companies who put their customers first.

We were suddenly in a new era of the social web. Now, brands are being forced to be more visual with their branding and be consistent with their content, specifically using SEO (search engine optimisation) and

SMO (social media optimisation). Doing this rewards your business with targeted traffic and a higher page ranking. But this means that to increase your chances of converting users to customers, your new website needs to look, feel and be used a little bit differently to three years ago. If you haven't done so already now is the time to update your website to reflect these exciting changes.

A clean, simple, fast and effective onsite experience often called a user-journey can be broken down into two important factors.

Firstly, the UX (User Experience), which is about how the user feels when they explore many different approaches to solving a specific user problem. The broad responsibility of the UX is to ensure the user flows logically from one step to the next. One way a UX might do this is by conducting in-person user tests to observe behaviour. By identifying content and visual stumbling blocks, you can refine your search to create the best user experience.

Secondly, unlike UX, which is concerned with the overall feel of the product, the UI (User Interface) is all about how the product is laid out. It is the design of each screen or page that a user interacts with and it ensures that the UI is visually communicating the path a UX has laid out.

To help you get a better understanding of this, ask yourself this. What do I want a user to do? Also, how do you want to communicate with them, by capturing their name or email or by getting them to buy your product or service? If you're still not clear, take a look at what your competitors are doing and go through the step-by-step process yourself. If you are finding this difficult, so will your user.

I have given you a brief overview of what Google has given us in terms of SEO for business. Now we can look further into SEO and really define what it is and how important it is for your business. SEO is the use of a search engine to affect the visibility of a website or a web page in a search engine's search results, whether this be natural or paid.

SEO Onsite

Search engine optimisation is all about making sure your online presence is visible to those who are most likely going to need your product or service. Understanding your business, target market and product/service is the foundation for marketing your business through online content using keywords. SEO can be broken down into two types: Onsite and Offsite. Onsite is defined as being optimisation within your website and includes; domain name, meta description, web content, internal links, title tags and keywords, rich media files, permalinks, outbound links, bounce rate and loading speed.

This list can be very confusing and I like to simplify it for you, so you can focus on the most crucial parts when constructing your website, using Google's latest algorithm. The most important aspects of SEO are your competitor analysis, keyword research, applying keywords and site speed.

To make sure you are building the right SEO strategy for your business, you need to either hire someone to help you do this, or learn from an expert and do it yourself. The best tool for your SEO research around your business and target customer is Google Adwords: Keyword Planner. This Google tool allows users to build a document based on keywords around their business and see based on monthly searches, how influential those keywords will be for your business.

To give you an example; one of my clients is a swimwear and clothing company, with different types of products, including; swimwear, lingerie, nightwear and active wear. Together we created an excel document with one tab labelled target customers and a further four tabs for each different product range.

We put in keywords for each product and keywords to describe the specific target market.

You can do the same for your business so it is accurately described through keywords and so you can move on to plan your website page map (the user journey you want to send your customers on when they come to your website home page). You want to be looking for keywords, which have low competition with high monthly search.

As soon as you have created an excel document for your business with at least 50 keywords for each tab, you can apply the data to your website and tell your own website story. If you are new to SEO and don't know what information you should be putting where on a basic level, keep reading.

As a business, you want to be at the top of the Google search engine as a result of using the right keywords. The higher you are on the search, the more likely you are to make sales. To continue telling the story, you need to make sure every page on your website is optimised, from a search engine perspective; otherwise your website will lose potential sales.

SEO Offsite

Offsite SEO is link building. Search engines will quantify a website's influence online based on what other online sources say about the site, which is where link building comes in. Along with link building, there are three other parts to offsite SEO you need to implement.

Link Building

A link building's campaign objective should be to have inbound links to your website from high quality and popular sources. Having quality links with regularly updated content are two sure fire ways to rank high in the search engines and drive more traffic to your website.

Competitor Analysis

There is no one better to learn from than your competitors. Analysing the way your competitors are doing their SEO will help you learn a great deal about your own business, whether this is through success or failures. Doing this will help you achieve the right outcome when developing your online marketing strategy. Looking at everything from their site architecture, keywords and inbound links will give you the knowledge you need to improve your own infrastructure.

Website Code

Coding constructs a website and this an important factor you need to consider when doing your SEO. The better the layout of the website and the easier the code is to read, the higher Google will rank you in their search.

Analytics

You must monitor the performance of your website. Without doing this, you won't be able to see how much traffic you are getting, sales you are receiving and many other important analytical factors. Running a regular analytical performance report will provide you with the data you need and I will give you a tool to do this in the next chapter.

Onsite and offsite SEO are very important steps in building a socially-savvy business, because without the correct SEO data on your website and link building in place, Google especially, won't rank your business higher than your competitors.

Google Keyword Research for SEO and SMO

To really understand your business and your target audience, you first need to know what keywords and phrases they are using when they search for products and services similar to yours.

Here is a step-by-step guide to set up your socially-savvy business, which will prepare you for content marketing.

1. Keyword spreadsheet (download from **thinkdigitalfirst.today**)

2. Sign up for Google Keyword Planner, to select keywords for your PPC campaign (if you're new to this you must fill in your details to access this free tool)

3. Click on tools and then keyword planner

4. It will ask you 'what would you like to do; click 'search for new keyword and ad group ideas'

5. You are given a few options. I recommend taking the url of a competitor and placing it into the 'your landing page' box and click 'get ideas'. This will give you a comprehensive list of keywords and phrases used on their website and used by an individual to search for the product/service. This is a great starting point, where you can take the keywords relevant to your business and place them in the keyword spreadsheet.

   a. Start with the word chosen

   b. Then the adgroup

   c. Take three words that appear in the adgroup (always making sure you are only taking the relevant keywords and phrases)

6. Continue to populate the Keyword spreadsheet using different tabs for:

   a. the business – overview of what the business does

   b. the target customer - list all the attributes of a target customer

   c. your specific products or services

7. Remember to add the amount of monthly searches along with how popular that keyword is.

You should now have an excel spreadsheet which is full of keywords that are all relevant to your business. Here is an example for a niche market bespoke kitchen designer.

SEO RESEARCH

Phrases	Keywords 1	Keyword 2	Keyword 3
Cabinet Making	Kitchen cabinets	Cabinet Design	kitchen cabinet designs
Cabinet Makers	Cabinet Maker	Bespoke Cabinet Maker	London Cabinet Maker
Kitchen Cabinet Makers	kitchen cabinets	wood kitchen cabinets	cabinet maker
Kitchen Cabinet Maker	Cabinet Maker	kitchen cabinet doors	solid wood cabinets
Bespoke Cabinet Makers	cabinet maker	cabinet makers london	Kitchen doors
Cabinet Makers London	cabinet makers london	Cabinet Maker London	free standing cabinets
Bespoke Furniture	Bespoke Furniture London	bespoke furniture makers	fitted wardrobes
Bespoke Kitchen	Bespoke Kitchens	Bespoke Kitchens London	kitchen units
Handmade	bespoke kitchens london	designer kitchens	kitchen units
Bespoke Kitchen Company	Bespoke Kitchens	bespoke kitchens london	handmade kitchen
Bespoke Handmade kitchen	handmade kitchens	bespoke kitchen design	bespoke kitchen
Bespoke English Kitchen	plain english kitchens	Bespoke Kitchens	plain english kitchen
Bespoke English Kitchens	plain english kitchens	Bespoke Kitchens	plain english kitchen
Bespoke London Kitchen	bespoke kitchens london	new kitchen	handmade kitchens
Bespoke London Kitchens	fitted kitchens london	bespoke kitchens	bespoke kitchen design
Bespoke shaker Kitchen	Bespoke Shaker kitchens	Shaker Kitchens	shaker style kitchen
Bespoke shaker Kitchens	shaker kitchens	shaker style kitchen	shaker kitchen
Fitted Furniture	fitted bedroom furniture	fitted bathroom furniture	fitted wardrobes
Fitted Kitchen	fitted kitchens	fitted kitchens london	Bespoke fitted kitchens
Fitted Kitchens	fitted kitchens uk	kitchen cupboard doors	Fitted Kitchen
Designer Fitted Kitchen	Designer Fitted Kitchen	fitted kitchens	designer kitchens
Designer Fitted Kitchens	Designer Fitted Units	fitted kitchens	designer kitchens
Designer Kitchens	designer kitchens	handmade kitchens	luxury kitchen designs
Marylebone Cabinet Makers	london marylebone	cabinet maker	quality kitchens
Marylebone Kitchen	kitchen marylebone	marylebone london	kitchen london
Marylebone Kitchens	handmade kitchens	bespoke kitchens	kitchen fitters
Marylebone kitchen designer	kitchens by design	kitchens direct	kitchens london
Marylebone designer kitchen	kitchen company	fitted kitchens	luxury kitchens

The next step is to take this information and define the metadata and page copy for each word and every page of your website, including your 'About' and 'Contact Us' pages.

To make sure you are staying page specific, you must decide which four keywords you want to stay consistent with for Google (metadata) and the consumer (on-page copy).

Here is an example (download from **thinkdigitalfirst.today**)

JACKETS AND COATS		
	Focus phrase	Casual Jackets for Women, Puffer Jackets and Women's Parkas
	Alt Img Text	Casual Jackets for Women, Puffer Jackets and Women's Parkas
	SEO Title	Jackets & Coats I Shop Casual Jackets for Women and Women's Parkas I BRAND.CO.UK
	Meta description	Shop relaxed women's parkas, puffer jackets and casual jackets for women from our selection of French and Italian labels at BRAND.CO.UK I Free Delivery to UK & Europe
	Landing Page Copy	From the ultimate navy blazer to a relaxed women's parka, you're sure to find the perfect cover-up from our selection of women's jackets and coats. Choose from ultra-sophisticated cuts by Extenzo and Cara Lotti or opt for Piomini's casual jackets for women.

Once you've completed the all-important pages of your website in this format, you need to go and apply it to the rest of your website. Remember to go to Google Webmaster and inform Google you've made changes to your website, so it can crawl and index all your new keywords.

In Chapter Six, I will share with you how to take these keywords and apply them to your content marketing strategy and integrate it into your digital communication, staying brand and keyword consistent.

Social Networks

Only a decade ago, social media was no more than a budding trend, introduced by MySpace, Bebo and Friendster. From 2005, Facebook changed the game. Twitter and LinkedIn increased the already impressive Facebook user database and Google+, Instagram, YouTube and Pinterest soon followed, plus some other brilliant new kids on the block, including: Vine, SnapChat, Ello and Plague. The future for brands is about understanding: why should I be using these networks? and how to engage as each network has its own USP; and what to say about your brand and industry.

As someone who has spent 10,000s of hours of my career connecting on social networks for personal and business, I can say being focused on SMO (social media optimisation) that compliments my SEO, has changed the way I've connected with people online and in a really good way, like nothing else in the history of marketing.

" KEEP BRAND AND TARGET AUDIENCE CONSISTENT
—— *through* ——
KEYWORDS "

For you to really understand how you can benefit from all of the social media platforms mentioned so far, right across free and paid advertising, I have highlighted the important things you need to know to apply a marketing budget to your campaigns.

FACEBOOK

Facebook is changing. It is not the network it used to be. This is the first thing you need to realise. Simply having a Facebook page or group and expecting people to find you; is not enough.

Just like Google, it has a unique algorithm that knows how often you use it and whether you are staying content consistent and engaging your audience with your brand message on a daily basis. It's call EdgeRank and when you do a relevant status update, it knows if your audience has liked, commented and shared your post. It ranks your page accordingly.

You will notice a few words I will keep repeating throughout this book and two of these are relevant and consistent.

Sharing updates, uploading pictures, asking friends and family to like your page along with posting on other pages and connecting with users are all free ways to use Facebook for your business. In Chapter Six, I'll be sharing with you a strategy to help grow your audience using a free and paid approach.

According to Facebook: *Most online advertising reaches only 27% of its intended audience. Facebook's average is 91%. Your business gets more value from every ad.*

According to an AdRoll (paid content distribution platform) analysis of ad impressions through Facebook ads in the newsfeed achieve 49-times higher click-through rates and a 54% lower CPC (in full) than traditional placements in the right-rail sidebar. To reach your customers on social media, promote your business right in the middle of the social sphere, there is no better place than the newsfeed. This is where 40% of Facebook users spend their time.

It can be hard to make sure your business is showing up in your fan's newsfeeds, so here are three ways you can help improve your Facebook newsfeed exposure.

1. Calculate your reach
You can easily calculate your Facebook Ad reach by visiting your Facebook insights. Look at your reach during the last 30 days and divide that by your fan count and this is your expected exposure.

2. Always Post Photos
Photos drive up to 20 times more interaction than a post with only text or a link. Photos are the most engaging type of content and are most likely to reach a higher audience than any other content.

3. Drive revenue
If you want to drive revenue run a competition, which will allow you to grow your fan base while converting customers. Competitions are great for visibility and even though you have to give away the prize, the revenue you can drive from doing this, is much more worthwhile.

TWITTER

Twitter is my personal favourite and best customer convertor for lead generation and sales.

With an average of 5,700 tweets being sent every second: how do you stand-out from the crowd and get your voice heard?

The first way to do this, free of charge is through the use of hashtags. Using the # before a word or phrase (with no spaces) makes it into a searchable keyword. The tweets with a hashtag are two times more likely to get engagement because people know how to listen into what they are interested in.

The second way to use Twitter as a business for free is to use Twitter Lists. A list is a group of Twitter users, which you or another user has created. Viewing a list will show you a stream of tweets from only the users on that list. These can be public or private.

In 2010, Twitter started a new trend in the native social media-advertising world when they introduced promoted tweets to users. Promoted tweets are those which advertisers have purchased to reach a wider group of users and to encourage engagement. You can tell the difference between promoted tweets because it is clearly labelled as Promoted. To help you use promoted tweets, here are five ways to help you build your exposure through Twitter's native advertising.

1. Promote Great Content
Your content needs to be engaging and interesting. Tweeting informational and inspirational posts is a great way to drive engagement. Even when you do promote a tweet, this isn't the end of your marketing on Twitter. You need to follow it up by being consistent with your tweets, making sure your content is sharable.

2. Events
When you run a promoted tweet, talk about an event you are running. This will make your ad time-based and exciting, making users take action.

3. Own Hashtags
Twitter advertising is a great way to introduce a hashtag you are using around your business or an event you are running. The tweet you are promoting must include keywords or phrases that are relevant to your business.

4. Geotargetting
Regardless of whether your business is operating in one specific area, you need to target an area where your demographic lives. Remember not to waste money on people who won't buy your product or service.

5. Encourage Action
Offer your readers immediate value if they click on your promoted tweet. You need to tell your readers how you can help them, rather than talking about how great you are. Make the action you want them to take clear and time-based.

Using Twitter's promoted tweets will allow you to grow your audience and generate leads. You can check your campaigns regularly so you are aware of what is working and what isn't. A/B (split test your ads) testing and measuring your results will give you the knowledge you need to either change your advertisement, or carry on with it.

LINKEDIN

Linked in.

LinkedIn is the largest B2B social network and boosts more than 300 million users. There are many ways you can use LinkedIn to market yourself and your business.

The first thing you must do is complete your profile up to 100%, by filling in all of your profile and getting recommendations. A quick tip for you to be seen on the first page in the search, you must place two keywords, which reflects who you are and what you do, in five separate places on your LinkedIn profile, as listed below.

1. Professional headline
2. Summary
3. Skills
4. Current job
5. Past job

By doing this, you are visible to LinkedIn's algorithm, you need to set up a business profile and ask all of your staff, stakeholders, Board members etc. to add their role to their profile. Start a group and getting involved in groups is a great way to connect with like-minded people and reach your target audience.

Sponsored updates allow you to raise awareness for your business and generate quality leads. Publishing content on LinkedIn is a great way to connect to business professionals who are already in your network. With sponsored updates, you can reach an even larger audience across multiple channels, including mobile.

Another way you can use LinkedIn's marketing solutions is by using their content advertisement tool. This is very similar to Facebook ads and will give you the platform to distribute content in multiple formats.

In September 2014, LinkedIn introduced a new marketing tool called long-form posting. This allows you to share your latest blogs and articles with your audience. I have seen amazing results using LinkedIn's long-form posting and know first-hand how great it can be to increase exposure and drive engagement.

PINTEREST

Pinterest is the fastest growing social network in history and is one of the most exciting platforms in the social sphere. Visual content is 40% more likely to encourage a customer to buy a product. Pinterest has definitely nailed this.

Looking at Pinterest, the organic growth of the network is extremely valuable, especially if your target market is female. Pinterest boasts 80% women who are positively engaged with brands on the site. This gives businesses with that target audience a great opportunity to reach consumers in one central place.

However, Pinterest is more than a social network for SMO, it is also really useful from a SEO perspective, because Google and Pinterest have a great relationship. When someone searches in Google for a 'white wedding dress' and click on the images tab, Google will bring images from Pinterest that have those specific keywords in the title and present them on the front page of Google. Once again free traffic to your brand.

To complement the importance of keywords and your SMO, earlier this year, Pinterest announced it had introduced promoted pins. This works in the same way as LinkedIn's promoted posts and Twitter's promoted tweets. While it is too early to see whether Pinterest's promoted pins drive more sales for a business, it is safe to say that the network is evolving every day and in my opinion, opportunities to grow a business on Pinterest are endless.

INSTAGRAM

Instagram

Instagram was launched on October 6th, 2010 and is one of the most innovative social networks, because sharing a photo or video using of hashtags results in better exposure than any other social network mentioned.

By the end of 2011, Instagram had hit the one million mark, seeing the likes of Starbucks and Marc Jacobs leading the way for businesses. It now claims 60 million photos are being shared on a daily basis.

On Instagram your brand's story will be surrounded by other beautiful content in a creative and inspiring environment. One of the unique features about Instagram, is that you can tell your story about the image by simply using hashtags. People search by hashtags, so the more relevant you are with your hashtags about the image and the brand, the easier it makes it for people find you.

Because it's a mobile only network, you can't use your desktop to save photos and share later. Or can you? In Chapter Five, I will share with you a tool that allows you to do that and in Chapter Six I talk about an Image Content strategy.

Here are five quick ways to get you started on Instagram.

1. Share a variety of content
Just because you want to increase sales, it doesn't mean every post has to be about this. Your community want relevant information from you that isn't just sales focused.

2. Timing is important
Regardless of how many users are on Instagram, timing is still important. There are popular times when users are more engaged with their community. Studies have shown that posting a picture between 9am and 9pm BST is going to give you the best results.

3. Hashtags are crucial
Hashtags have a huge impact on how successful your Instagram post is. Also, Instagram is a search tool and hashtags compliment this perfectly. Connect with unconnected users by including relevant hashtags in your posts.

4. Video functionality
Instagram allows users to post photos and videos. Using a video to share information about your business allows users to connect with you on a more personal level.

5. Filters are key
Using a filter on one of your Instagram photos is a great way to give your image a more professional and edgy feel, as well as increasing the number of likes you will receive. The top three most effective filters are Normal or No Filter, Mayfair and Inkwell.

Just like all the other social networks you can also sponsor images and videos to your target audience.

Here's what Instagram say:
Everyone on Instagram will see ads from time to time whether or not they're Facebook users, and basic information from Facebook helps create a more relevant experience. Providing feedback if you see an ad you don't find interesting will also help us show you more engaging ads over time.

Applying a natural and paid strategy to your campaign will increase your brand awareness and conversion.

YOUTUBE

YouTube has four billion views per day and you won't find these stats on any other network. Brought by Google in 2006, YouTube is the second largest search engine in the world and holds more video content than any other website in the universe. As I've previously mentioned, optimising your content (SMO) in YouTube will also drive natural traffic from Google (SEO).

YouTube is free and the basics still apply. Set up a strong and brand consistent page from a visual and content perspective, so when you upload photos, add descriptions, keywords and categories based on your industry sector, it will be searchable to the user. If you want to advertise, this is where it gets interesting.

YouTube ads are set up through Google's advertising hub. However, it works slightly differently. When you set up YouTube ads, you only pay when someone choses to watch your ad. This can be a lot more valuable than a click through if you are using the right content in your video.

Here are 10 tips to help you use YouTube for your business.

1. Keep introducing new content
2. Include calls to action
3. Customise your channel
4. Speak to your viewers through comments
5. Test your titles
6. Chose the right category and tags
7. Consider collaborating
8. Use subtitles
9. Write an engaging description
10. Share your videos on other social networks as well.

Google+

Google+ has been quoted as the 2nd biggest social network. It's one that's easily forgotten but often for the wrong reasons. Offering images, videos, content, communities and much more, it stands side by side with some of the longer running networks, which offer the same type of features.

As a small business, what do you want to get from using Google+?

In my opinion, you need to include it in your overall marketing mix, from a branding and SMO and SEO perspective. Yes, it's possible to build a community if you already have a large client base and database, which use Google+.

The newly named Google Business offers business owners a suite of tools to help build the presence of your online brand, from places, to events, photos to video, live streaming via hang outs. In Chapter Six, I will share with you a strategy, which got me on the front page of Google using my Google+ account based on target keywords.

Whatever social network you decide is right for your personality, your business or where your target audience hang out, always make sure you put your best foot forward and Think #Digital First. Give the user an experience they will fall in love with, over and over again and remember to always add your social icons in your various online profiles, including your website. Also, have your social media links on your printed literature from business cards and leaflets to banners at all public events and tradeshows.

Digital Marketing

Posting an update on Facebook, sending a tweet on Twitter, uploading a pin on Pinterest, sending out a Google+ or LinkedIn update and sharing a photo on Instagram are organic ways to drive social media traffic. Social media is just one of many ways to drive organic traffic. To really make the most of generating traffic online, you need to consider digital marketing as a whole.

Digital marketing is the marketing of products or services using a number of different digital channels to reach new and current consumers. The main objective of digital marketing is to promote your business through your digital media.

Digital marketing is more than what you see online. It extends to offline channels, including: SMS and MMS. It requires a whole new approach and understanding of customer behaviour. You need to analyse the value of every action from a tweet and Facebook like to mobile activity.

Digging deeper into digital marketing, here are a few ways to continue your two-way online engagement by running competitions, doing email marketing, blogging and utilising the power of bloggers through influencer marketing and connecting with your target audience in forums and communities. Running a webinar is a great way to add value to your audience and enables you to share the value of your business to a large group of people from the comfort of your office or home (as I do on a monthly basis).

Competitions
To run a competition on any social media network, you first need to choose a third party application, which has been verified, especially on Facebook. Running a competition using the online stream without a third party application breaks Facebook's rules and they will close your page down over night. I will share a great tool for you to use in the next chapter. You need to think about what you are offering and what you want in return. Are you going to give a product away for free and in return ask for a name and email address? Attractive images, videos and descriptions will need to be included so you can draw your target market in.

Email Marketing
If you decide to run a competition and ask for a name and email address, your end goal for this should be to use it as part of your email marketing strategy. Lead generation is one of the best ways to build your email database. However, you should never buy lists unless they have been 100% qualified. Delivering highly relevant

content is a strategic goal, which 67% of marketers say their business wants to achieve through email marketing.

Here are five things to consider for your email marketing.

1. Make email marketing part of your customer acquisition journey
2. Use mobile optimisation
3. Use personalised templates
4. Give away great content and value
5. Know what you are going to share

Blogging

Some small businesses don't have the budget needed to run advertisements and one of the only ways they can digital market their business is by blogging. There is some debate as to whether blogging is still as important as it used to be and I can say for certain, it is.

I write two blogs on my Warren Knight website every week and the first is posted on Tuesday (#TechTuesday), the second on a Friday as per my online marketing strategy. It has been one of the best ways to validate myself as an influencer in my industry. If you struggle to write or can't think of a title don't worry, I am going to share with you a tool to help you with this in Chapter Five.

Marketing has evolved into a P2P (person to person) relationships rather than the usual B2C (business to customer) or B2B (business to business). The latest craze coming from the digital world is Bloggers Outreach. Publishing your message out to people is no longer enough. You need to make a connection with consumers and tell them about yourself.

Bloggers typically have an advantage when it comes to spreading a message online because they have direct access to your target audience and can influence sales through word of mouth.

Research from BlogHer showed that 81% of the online population trusts information and advice they get from bloggers and 61% have made a purchase based on a blogger's recommendation.

There are many ways to get bloggers talking about your brands, products or services and here are five things to help you.

1. Do your research; know who the blogger is before you ask them to write about your business.

2. Do tell the truth; be honest in your opening email to a blogger and tell them exactly who you are and what you are looking to do. Credibility goes a long way online.

3. Do be respectful; never appear rude or hostile because this will only influence the blogger to talk about you in a negative way online.

4. Do send a gift; a thank you for writing about my business goes a long way and it will help you build a relationship with that blogger.

5. Do be unique; create unique and quality content that will be engaging.

Content Marketing

Content marketing is creating and distributing valuable content across multiple channels using keywords to talk about the brand, product, service and target customer. Did you know that 61% of consumers prefer companies with custom online content?

• Articles
Writing articles and blogging should be a key part of your Content Marketing Strategy. Writing blogs about your business and relevant industry content is one way to drive traffic to your website through content marketing.

• Infographics
An infographic is a visual representation of information about a certain topic. There are many great tools to help you create an infographic free of charge, which I will share in the next chapter. Make sure the content you include in your infographic is sharable and visually stimulating. The better the layout and the colours, the more it will catch peoples' attention.

• Whitepapers

A whitepaper is a report or guide written by an authoritative figure, which helps users understand a topic or solve an issue. Writing a whitepaper as part of your Content Marketing Strategy is a great way to boost your online profile as a thought leader in your industry.

• Guest blogging

I am a guest blogger for two highly influential platforms; Social Media Today and Business2Community. They both sit in my industry sector and allow me to post worthy content to drive social media activity and build my online profile.

• Repurposing content

All these ways to content market don't need to be used just once. You can repurpose your content. Creating an infographic once will allow you to share via all your social channels, email marketing and even on your blog. One piece of content can flow out to multiple sources.

Once you have your content ready to market, you need to amplify it. Chapter Five is about tools to help your business grow and when it comes to amplification, there are some great tools you can use to help you save time.

Paid Advertisement

If you decide that you want to spend money on native advertising, you can do so through PPC which means you will pay for every designated click you receive to your website.

Google

The holy grail of advertising comes from the largest search engine in the world, Google. Introduced in October 2000, Google advertising has allowed businesses to improve their search engine ranking for a small fee via PPC advertising. Google Adwords generated £10.33 billion in revenue in Q4 of 2013, which shows that businesses are seeing the benefits from using Google as an advertising platform. Expect to pay on average £1.53 per click for an advertisement (this may vary depending on your niche).

This is why you should be using Google Adwords for your business.

1. Measurable and Flexible

Online marketing and specifically Google Advertising is very easy to measure. Thanks to Google's other great tools, including Google Analytics you can measure how your website is performing and also it has its own PPC metrics which will give you all the information you need.

2. Faster than SEO

One of the biggest problems with search engine optimisation is that it can take months before you see any drastic results. With the use of Google AdWords, you will get instant results as soon as you set your campaign live.

3. Engaging

Google have introduced new advertising formats, which give users a more engaging experience by using image and in-video advertisement.

4. Full control over advertising costs

The same as on Facebook, you set a maximum cost per click for each day of your advertising campaigns. If you only have £100 to spend, Google will not go over this allowance and will give you the data you need to decide whether your advertisement is driving the right amount of traffic.

5. Get the upper hand on your competitors

Using AdWords gives you an advantage over your competitors because of how quickly it works. According to Moz 80% of search results now contain AdWords ad placements.

6. ReMarketing adverts

ReMarketing is showing ads to users who have previously visited your website as they are browsing your web. Doing this is one of the best ways to reach your target market, more than once.

Bing

Google isn't the only search engine. Microsoft's Bing controls more than 25% of the world's search engines, mainly because countries such as China have banned the use of Google. You might decide you want to focus more time optimising your site for Bing and the good news is that its algorithm is similar to Google's in many ways. These have a large number of high-quality backlinks and also, they optimise urls and domain names for keywords. However, there are some things you need to consider when optimising your website for Bing.

Bing favours older websites with more official domain names, for example .edu or .gov. Bing also knows how to index flash media (unlike Google) and Bing has a stronger attachment to showing small business results rather than bigger businesses. Google and YouTube are the two biggest search engines in the world and in my opinion Bing's popularity isn't substantial enough to focus a lot of time and effort on.

<u>Advertising on Amazon</u>

Amazon is the largest selling product service in history and has now made it easier for businesses to get better exposure through their product advertisement tool.

All you need to do is upload your products using Amazon's user-friendly tool, decide on a budget and set your product live. Your advertisement will be targeted at shoppers searching for related items on the Amazon website. Your ad will be seen in detailed pages, search results and the buy box. As soon as a potential customer clicks on your advertisement, they will be taken to the product page on your website.

Amazon will only charge you when a shopper clicks on your advertisement and reaches your website. This is known as CPC (cost per click). The amount you pay is based on your initial bid. As the customer ends up on your website to purchase your product, you are in complete control of the branding and user purchasing experience. This is a great way to capture leads while increasing sales.

Public Relations

Public Relations (PR) is the management of information being shared between a person and an organisation as a way to boost the profile of an individual or business. If you are looking to launch your business and want extra exposure for your product or service, the best way to reach those who are influential and might write about your business is through PR. If you don't know how to write a press release, here are some pointers to help you.

- Keep the headline of the Press Release relevant, clear and to the point.

- Use the keywords within your business to help you with this.

- Use a larger font for your headline because it is the first thing people read.

- Capture the feel of the press release in the first sentence of your main body text.

- Have the date and the city your company is based in, in the body text.

- Keep it simple to read and easy to understand. Avoid using long sentences as well as fancy language.

- Sum up the press release in the first paragraph and the rest of the text should elaborate on this.

- Use the five Ws (Who, What, When, Where and Why) to write your press release. Make sure you have information on each W in your document.

- Provide information links to support your press release.

- Include information about your company and contact details at the end of the press release, for the people who want to find out more.

If you know from Chapter Three that writing isn't a strength of yours and your time is better spent elsewhere, you can hire someone to do this for you.

Affiliate Marketing

Affiliate marketing is, in essence a sales strategy. An individual will share links to your products and receive a commission when they get a sale. This is otherwise known as Performance Marketing. The 2010 IAB Internet Advertising Revenue Report (www.iab.net/adrevenuereport) showed that affiliate advertising accounted for 62% of Internet ad revenues. This has changed because of the increase in businesses using social media advertising. However, Affiliate Marketing should not be ignored.

To make your Affiliate Marketing a success, you need to be able to communicate. This needs to be regular, especially with key affiliates and clear, concise and straight to the point. This process teamed with planning, clear commercials, great product feeds and banners along with incentives and promotions are what will make your Affiliate Marketing a success.

To have a totally socially-savvy business, where you have thought about every sales and marketing opportunity, utilising everything I have mentioned in this chapter, takes time. It takes weeks of preparation, implementation and analysing the results to make sure you are always increasing your brand awareness, lead generation and ultimately sales. Take baby steps and each day focus on achieving a small goal, which always moves the business forward.

Entering Awards

A great way to market your business, build your profile in your industry, get accreditations and have something to talk about via a press release and across social media is to enter local, industry and business awards.

In one of my start-up technology companies we won many awards and also were highly recommended in others and this quickly built a name for our business in our industry, simply by focusing on writing a great story and spending a few hundred pounds on entering the awards.

I have had the pleasure of being a judge at various digital marketing and technology awards and because of this, I wanted to share with you, a few helpful tips. There are some very simple questions that need answering, however, the answers are not as easy as they seem. Firstly, which awards should you enter?

Never wait until an organisation approaches you to enter their awards procedure. Create a plan, know which awards you are going to enter before they accept entrants and be prepared for the difficult questions. Here are some things to ask yourself before entering:

1. How much of your marketing budget have you allocated to entering awards?
2. What do you want the award to say about your business?
3. Are you focusing on local (regional), national or international awards?
4. When are you going to be ready to tell your story?
5. Be ready to PR and Market once you have won.

It sounds great to enter every single award in your industry in the hope that you get shortlisted for at least half, but think about the cost. Entries are usually priced between £50 - £750 and that doesn't include the night of the awards, which will most likely cost between £99 - £500 for just one seat.

To be fully prepared to enter an award, have a planning session with the people around you. Know your story, build up a file of case studies and have short but intelligent answers to potential questions. Winning an award is not easy and it usually depends on how well you have presented your business in a written or verbal presentation.

About 20% of awards are not just based on a written entry. There is usually a second stage which is a presentation of some form to a panel of judges with a Q and A. This is a lot more challenging than a written entry, so make sure you know which awards require this from you and be as prepared as possible.

In Chapter Six, I'll be talking about your 90-day Marketing Plan, where all of these actions can be planned out and executed with laser focus precision.

FIVE

TOOLS TO MAKE YOUR BUSINESS GROW

#NOONECANDOITBETTER

I have spent the last seven years researching and learning many management tools to help me grow my business knowledge. I've come across and used 100s of different online tools and it can be pretty overwhelming. So, I will share with you the best that I have found, researched, tested and used effectively in each category. This chapter is about knowing the tools you need for different aspects of your business. I have focused on the ones that in my opinion are the most intelligent whatever stage your business is at now #NoOneCanGoItBetter

The first set of tools I want to share with you, are those that help you research and listen to your customers and competitors.

1. Researching and Listening

Addict-o-matic: allows you to create a web page filled with content from search engines and social networks. As a business, it can be hard to manage your time and when it comes to marketing, you need to be able to gather information online suitable for your audience.

Alltop: if you don't know where to find your sources or influencers, check out Alltop. It was built by Guy Kawasaki and is a great website to find articles based on your industry sector.

Browser Folder (Bookmark): this is a browser folder you can create in your internet browser as a great place to save website urls for a later date. Think of it as your online filing cabinet.

FEEDLY

Feedly: allows you to find online content and keep it in one place. If you have websites you want to save visually in an organised way, this is the tool for you. I use it on a daily basis.

Google Alerts: use this tool to keep an eye on what is being posted online about your business. Be warned, it may take a while for you to receive an email from Google sharing the latest mentions around your keywords. But this is a useful platform to listen to what is being said about you, your business for brand reputation and your competitors online.

Social Mention: for real time searches across all social networks, Social Mention is a great tool to use. Enter in any business or individual name and see how they have been mentioned across various different networks online.

Twellow: this is the yellow pages of Twitter where you can search for influential people in your industry and follow them. You can also increase your followers' list by using this tool.

2. Business

Building a business and understanding the online world can be difficult. With the help of the following tools, I can delegate tasks, save time and create a business that is fully integrated from offline to online. If you want to find someone to delegate work to virtually, here are three websites you can use and a tool to help keep track of them.

Freelancer: if you are looking for programmers, web developers, designers or writers, try freelancer. You can hire skilled professionals at a fraction of the usual cost and Freelancer is the world's largest outsourcing marketplace.

oDesk: is similar to Freelancer and gives you a database of savvy business and professional freelancers to work with. There are more than 45,000 UK businesses, which already use oDesk to hire and manage freelancers online. This is a great place to find the right expertise for your business.

People Per Hour: this is a great website to use if you are looking for professional visual work to be done for your business. Prices will be fixed by the freelancers and will be on a per hour basis.

Once you have your Virtual Assistant doing the required work for you, you will need... HubStaff.

HubStaff: is a tool I use to track how efficiently my Virtual Assistants are working. HubStaff includes great time tracking software with screenshots, activity levels, timesheets and reports. This is a complete tracking software, so you know your staff are working to a high standard.

When it comes to your website and marketing content, there are websites that have been specifically designed to help you with your content ideas.

Blog Idea Generator: this website has its own blog post Idea Generator. Have you ever been stuck trying to come up with an idea for your blog and wasted valuable time? This tool is very easy to use. However, it might not provide you with enough inspiration based on your industry sector.

Blog Topic Generator: Hubspot has been mentioned more than once and has helped me when I need to come up with a topic for my weekly blog. All you have to do is give the tool three nouns and it will give you five blog titles.

Portent's Content Idea Generator: will give you a great blog title and will explain why they have chosen certain key words based on what online users are most likely to click on. This will help you decide on the right keywords to use for present and future blogs.

Soovle: is a customisable engine that lets you search any keyword or phrase across all of the internet's top providers including Google, Bing, Amazon, YouTube and Wikipedia in one, central place.

Subject Line Gold: is one of my favourite tools for email marketing. It is critically important to come up with the perfect email subject line because this will ultimately affect the open and click rate of your emails. This tool predicts the results of your campaign, based on your subject line and will offer you suggestions of how to improve your subject line.

Ubersuggest: if you are looking for keyword ideas, Ubersuggest will do this for you and all you need to do is give it a term and it will do it's magic. It will save you so much time and provide you with great keywords. It also searches shopping news and video sites.

One of the biggest problems entrepreneurs face is finding the time to share information with the people they work with. Here are four of the best collaboration tools I have come across.

DROPBOX

Dropbox: is a cloud storing application that allows you to store files away from your computer. You can create folders and invite those you work with into the folders so they can see and use your files.

Google Docs: if you need to collaboratively work on a word document or excel spreadsheet, use Google Docs. You can invite someone into a document and it allows for more than one person to work on a document at one time. You can also set up a survey; design a presentation and much more.

HighriseHQ: is a CRM (Customer Relationship Manager), which helps you keep track of all your business contacts and the conversations you are having with potential customers and channel partners. Also you can group contacts and set up alerts so you never forget to call someone back. If HighriseHQ is not feature rich enough, try Nutshell, Capsule or Insightly.

TRELLO

Trello: helps you keep track of everything from pictures, articles and notes to important information and to-do-lists. Everything can be colour coded and it also allows you to collaborate with those you work with on projects to make sure progress can be tracked.

In Chapter Two, I spoke about managing your time and how important it is to keep focused and save time. Here are some of the best tools to help you save time.

Evernote: allows you to keep all your work in one place. It integrates with your Gmail so you can save emails and never have to waste time trying to find an important email ever again Evernote also syncs with Remember the Milk, which is a task management tool.

Focus Booster: is one of the best time productivity management tools around and is completely free to use. It is based on a pomodoro technique, which breaks tasks up into 25 minute intervals, allowing you to be productive in a time-based way. It is a great visual tool with a sleek looking application.

Meet Carrot: is a more visually appealing time management tool which you can use to create to-do lists, set alarms and even manage your workouts. It is great for the procrastinators, who need something to keep them focused on important tasks.

Pocket: is another time saving tool which allows you to pocket something for a later date. Also it automatically syncs to your phone, tablet or computer so you can view it at any time, regardless of whether you have an internet connection.

Moving on to the more technical side of the business, here are three different website builders.

SQUARESPACE

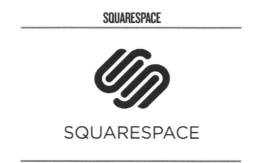

SQUARESPACE

Squarespace: offers a number of different options to create your website. They are simple to create, look professional and great on mobile. They also have an online store builder.

Wix: is an easy to use website builder because no coding skills are needed. It has more than 56 million users, with 100s of customisable templates.

WORDPRESS

WORDPRESS

Wordpress: in my opinion is one of the best website builders around. There is so much you can do with Wordpress and it's easy to use, with a number of free templates.

If you are looking to sell products online, you need an online store builder, which you can use on a subscription-based service. Here are some of the best.

BigCommerce: is an eCommerce platform, which I have spent a lot of time working with for clients. It has everything you need to create a fully integrated, professional looking online store.

Shopify: gives you a free 14-day trial before you pay for their monthly service. It has so many amazing features from customisation, analytics integration and discount options to search engine optimisation and unlimited products.

SupaDupa: is a great website builder, based in the UK. It has slick designs, easy customisation and is perfect for a business that has more than two variations for a product. Also, it includes; search engine optimisation, high-resolution product images and more than 45+ forward thinking themes.

Once you have built your website or online store, you need to look at which payment gateways you can use.

PAYPAL

P PayPal

PayPal: is one of the most popular ways to send and receive money online. Most websites and online store builders integrate with PayPal very easily and it processes more than 10 million payments, daily.

Skrill: is for businesses that need to accept easy, cost effective global payments. You can customise the platform so your consumers have a smooth payment experience, regardless of whether they are using a PC, tablet or smartphone.

Stripe: is a great gateway as an option to Paypal and you can give your customers options when they are purchasing from you. With Stripe there is no need to design payments from scratch, as they offer customisable payment processes, which your customers will love.

I have already shared with you some great listening and researching tools, as well as tools you need for your business. Now it is time to give you a few design tools to make your life easier.

3. Design/Visual

Animoto: is used to create professional looking videos for free, with a slideshow feel and with backing music. These videos can then be placed on platforms like Vimeo and YouTube.

CANVA

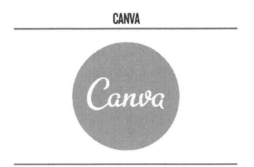

Canva: is deemed as good as Photoshop by some of the best designers in the industry. With great features and already existing images to use, you can create a professionally looking image in a matter of seconds.

PicMonkey: is a great image creation which I have been using for a long time. If you want to add some text to an already existing tool free of charge, PicMonkey is for you.

Snapseed: if you want to adjust and add filters to your photos, this is the smartphone app for you. It is convenient on-the-go and can be fun at the same time.

Visual.ly: is one of the best tools to use when you want to create an infographic. With existing templates, you just need to do your research and find great information and you can have a great piece of marketing material in less than an hour.

99designs: if you are time short and have decided that you can't focus on the designing side of your business, use this tool to find someone to help you. There is a process you need to go through which is run through a competition with an uploaded brief. You can be inundated with hundreds of designs to choose from. Your favourite design is the winner of the competition.

Video is just as important as images from a marketing perspective and here are a few websites where you can share videos.

YouTube: is the world's second largest search engine and one of the best places to share your videos. I have spoken about YouTube in an earlier chapter, but I had to include it as one of your must-use websites. A more business focused video-sharing platform is Vimeo.

Vine: is one of the hottest networks around and the best way to share life in motion. The videos are no longer than 30 seconds and are easily shareable on social media. Owned by Twitter, Vine's app can be used to browse through videos posted by other users. Also, it can be used with groups of videos by theme and trending videos, allowing you to categorise your videos based on your business sector.

The next set of tools and websites I am going to share with you are marketing based and can help you build your online profile.

4. Marketing

Gravatar: is an account every entrepreneur should have because it is simple to create and is an image that follows you from site to site appearing beside your name when you comment or post on a blog.

Klout: can be used to discover how influential you are online within your social media community. Anything more than 60 means you are in the top 5%. It is a website and mobile application that ranks users based on it's social influence on a numerical scale from 1 to 100.

To amplify your message across social media, take a look at the following tools.

HOOTSUITE

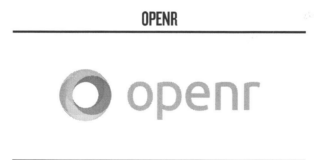

Hootsuite: I have been using Hootsuite for many years and cannot recommend it enough. It is one of the best amplification tools out there, allowing you to integrate with your social networks and schedule in advance.

OPENR

Openr: allows you to connect with your target audience by sharing relevant content. Openr gives you the tools to share unique content through a pop-up window with a message and call-to-action. This is a great way to showcase your latest product/service.

Schedugram: is used to manage multiple Instagram accounts, as well as scheduling images, which also saves you time.

SocialOomph: is similar to Hootsuite because it enables you to easily schedule posts to go out on your social network accounts. It also helps you monitor your activity and find quality people in your industry to follow.

ViralWoot: is specifically for Pinterest, and is a scheduling tool, as well as providing you with analytical information, pin alerts and management of multiple Pinterest accounts. It is used by more than 30,000 individuals and businesses giving you everything you need from a management and analytical perspective.

As a business, you should be looking at as many ways as possible to generate customer leads and drive campaign traffic. One of the best ways to do this is by running a competition. Here are some tools that will help you.

Gleam: is a great tool to run competitions, capture emails and offer rewards to your customers from one central place. It takes into account actions with real users when building a campaign to engage with others.

SHORTSTACK

Shortstack: allows you to drive traffic to your campaign from anywhere on the web. It is also a great plug-in for a Facebook Business Page. Shortstack allows you to create various campaigns as well as serving as a marketing hub for your business.

Slideshare: is slightly different because it is more of a presentation application, rather than a video sharing site. If you use power point presentations, PDFs, Case Studies, White Papers and eBooks that you want the world to see, use Slideshare.

WISHPOND

wishpond

Wishpond: is a third party application where you can run competitions on social media platforms, specifically Facebook. You can also create landing pages, run contests and promotions, as well as creating forms, pop-ups, ads and email campaigns.

There are many ways you, as a business can engage with your consumers. Here are three tools to help you converse in real time, run a meeting via a webinar and conduct a survey.

Gotowebinar: is a piece of software which I have used for years, it allows me to run monthly webinars to more than 100 people. It comes with a 30-day free trial and allows you to customise and record your webinars, so your customers can watch it in their own time.

SURVEYMONKEY

SurveyMonkey: is a great tool to use when you want to run a survey to get feedback on your latest product/service. Also, you can analyse results to see which options were chosen the most frequently and it is free of charge. Google Form is another option for you.

ZOPIM

Zopim: is a free, live, chat software which allows you to engage with consumers in real-time using a messenger-like website plug-in. This is a much faster and more personal way to connect with your consumers who have queries in real-time.

The next three tools I am going to share with you can help with your inbound marketing and automation.

Hubspot: is an inbound marketing and sales platform which helps companies to attract visitors, convert leads and close customers. Their features include; blogging, social media, SEO, landing pages, CRM, analytics and much, much more.

Marketo: provides easy and powerful marketing automation software, including everything from; email marketing, inbound marketing, content marketing, social marketing, customer engagement marketing, real-time personalisation and lead management.

Moz: builds tools that make inbound marketing easy, backed by industry-leading data and the largest community of SEOs on the planet. It gives you the tools to measure website rankings, social traffic, website and SEO errors, as well as opportunities, research and custom reporting.

Email marketing, as you would have read in the previous chapter, is one of the most crucial parts of your digital marketing strategy. Keep reading, if you don't know which tool to use.

Constant Contact: is a complete package, which includes email marketing, social media marketing, online surveys, event marketing, digital storefronts and local deals tools. Their tool kit gives you everything you need to create a great email marketing strategy and comes with a free trial.

Infusionsoft: with 23,000 small business users, this is a preferred tool used by many online marketers. It comes with a high monthly fee and takes a little getting used to, but it is highly effective if you have the budget. Features include; automation, website building and the ability to increase sales, while staying organised and focused.

MAILCHIMP

MailChimp

Mailchimp: is the world's leading email marketing tool and offers great templates, analytics, autoresponder, list creation, and personalisation, completely free of charge (unless you have more than 2,000 contacts).

Content marketing is just as important for your business as digital marketing. Here are four tools to help you organise your content, ready for your strategy.

Outbrain: is an advertising platform with one of its main features focusing on content marketing, helping publishers increase web traffic. Other features include amplification and advanced testing to boost your conversion rate.

Reddit: is a well-known entertainment and news website, with a large community of members who submit content for other users to read and share.

StumbleUpon: is otherwise known as a discovery engine, which holds a large collection of web content, created based on a user's interests. Look no further, if you want great, relevant and specific content.

Triberr: is an influencer marketing platform, where bloggers and online thought leaders come together to share great content.

In Chapter Six, I will share with you a strategy to help you implement the next set of tools which focus on your SEO.

5. Analytics Dashboards

When it comes to analytics, I have three great dashboards that you can download from my website, they are:

•   eCommerce: gives you clarity on which items are the best sellers;

•   lead generation: shows you which pages are converting the best for you and where the user is coming from; and

•   social media dashboard: tells you where your traffic is coming from.

The next four tools I am going to share with you, focus on which tools to use to measure your website traffic and data. For real time analytics, take a look at these tools.

Google Analytics: is the first choice for most small businesses when it comes to analytical data and analysis. You will need a Gmail account.

GOSQUARED

GoSquared: is the real-time analytics service that helps you act now, not tomorrow. You will have access to a trend dashboard, eCommerce analytics and a breakdown of what is happening in your website now. You can get a free trial with GoSquared followed by a monthly fee.

GTmetrix: helps you develop a faster, more efficient and all-round improved website experience for your users. Features include, tracking the history of your website, analysis on mobile devices, testing from multiple regions, monitored alerts, page loading playbacks and much, much more.

KissMetrics: is a person-based analytical platform for your business, where you can optimise your marketing, increase conversion rates and find new customers.

<u>6. SEO/Meta Data</u>

Google Adwords Keyword Planner: is one of the best tools coming from Google's empire. This helps you generate all the keywords you need for your website and your content marketing.

Spyfu: exposes some of the search marketing secrets from your most successful competitors. You can download your competitor's profitable keywords, for every domain and the places where they have shown up online.

Yoast: is a Wordpress plugin that allows you to optimise every web page and blog post on your website. It will rate your SEO on a traffic light system (red, orange and green).

There are many other online tools available and I am sure they are all good tools to use, but I had to draw the line somewhere, otherwise you'd be here all day searching.

SIX

STRATEGY & IMPLEMENTATION

#PUSHIT

In the last five chapters, I've helped you to understand a new mind set, given you the tips and tools to help save and protect your time, and automate your marketing process while focusing on sales to prepare your business for success. Now let the fun begin by taking all of your learning and putting it into action, so you can help more customers solve their pain with your product and service #PushIt.

To make sure you and your team are prepared for every eventuality, you need a strategy and an actionable plan.

Doing your homework on a prospective customer is crucial. There is no point picking up the phone to make a sales call, without knowing how to fully express the benefits of your product in the right way, so your customer responds positively. It is important that you know your pricing structure, based on selling different quantities, so you are not caught off guard when your customer requests this.

To help you, here is a simple four-step process and diagram. Using this will make sure you always know the steps you are taking are in the right direction, at the right time.

1. Go to Market Strategy

2. Marketing Plan

3. Sales Process

4. Customer Retention

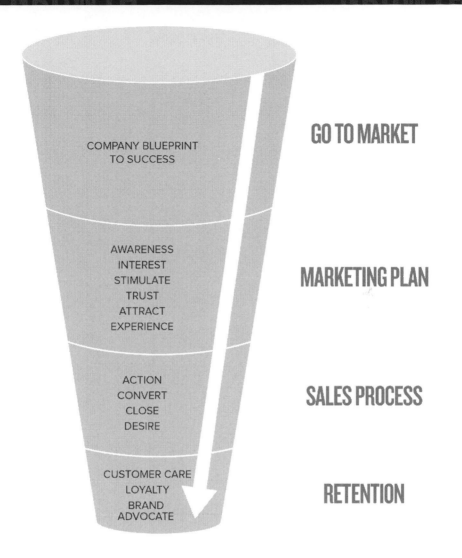

COMPANY BLUEPRINT
TO SUCCESS

GO TO MARKET

AWARENESS
INTEREST
STIMULATE
TRUST
ATTRACT
EXPERIENCE

MARKETING PLAN

ACTION
CONVERT
CLOSE
DESIRE

SALES PROCESS

CUSTOMER CARE
LOYALTY
BRAND
ADVOCATE

RETENTION

Step One: your Go to Market Strategy

Are you a business selling B2B (business to business) and or B2C (business to consumer) or a company, which only works through organisations who sell direct to your specific target audience on your behalf?

Here is an example. Basekit (an online store builder) has a business model where they do not have onboard any clients themselves. They only work with selective channel partners who already have their target audience engaged.

At the other end of the spectrum is being the one company, which everyone speaks to. For example: Richard Branson, he's a front facing brand and you connect to Virgin because of him, his branding and his market positioning.

On a small business scale, look at Levi Roots. He had an idea and passion to create a simple sauce and now he is worth more than £30 million. This is because of who he is and how his consumers have connected to his story.

You need to understand that you and your business are unique and the right process for you, might not work for another, even if you are in the same business sector. Unfortunately, it is common to see the wrong business models within organisations and hopefully, if this is you, you will benefit from the penultimate step of creating a socially-savvy business.

Your company's situation is different from your competitors and as customers (taking our business hats off for a moment) we have evolved the www into this amazing new social web. It gives you a voice to openly talk about your positive experiences, making brands listen and changing the way they do business.

So when it comes to marketing your brand. It's no longer as simple as the old AIDA sales process, which you have been using since 1904, as follows:

- building **Awareness;**

- gaining the **Interest;**

- sharing the **Desire;** and

- getting the user to take **Action.**

These days you want more from your customers, you want loyalty, and you want them to talk about your brand, to become brand advocates. At each stage of your Go to Market Strategy you want them to buy from you. Whether this is an impulse buy in real time, or a well thought through process that's taken months of research... it still matters.

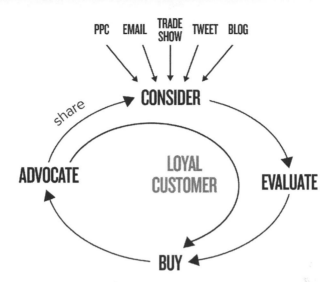

Go to Market Strategy

This is your company's blueprint, from which your overall sales and marketing plan evolves. Your business will share the value of its product or service by connecting with your laser targeted customers.

When deciding on your Go to Market Strategy, you need to include various revenue streams, which can flow into your business. This will determine how you communicate your message to your target customer. Your Go to Market Checklist will include the following.

- Solving a need in the market which offers fast growth

- Understanding your opportunity in the market

- Knowing who your laser focused target market is for initial launch

- Identifying the influencers in your industry to be brand advocates

- Understanding the pain point which will help you know what the business problem is and develop a unique selling proposition to solve it

- Discovering how you can be different from your competitors

- Preparing a product roadmap from idea to delivery

- Tracking and measuring your results

- Developing a sales and marketing plan integrated with a customer retention strategy

- Training your team in every aspect of the business process

- Identifying channel partners based on your target audience

- Completing your USP

When sharing the same USP with two different target customers you must offer a different value proposition to help them understand what pain your problem solves and how it can help them.

Next, you need to design an actionable plan in the form of a document which lists what steps must be taken and by whom to achieve a specific goal.

Marketing

Marketing is in essence, identifying, anticipating and meeting the requirements of what consumers want, to make a profit in your business. Putting the customers' wants and needs first will be identified through your market research.

Because your competitors might have the same target market as you it doesn't mean they are ultimately solving their pain. You must be carrying out research to find out what your target market really wants from your specific business.

Ask your customers about your product or service. What improvements would they like to see? Once you know this, you can develop a range of products or services, suitable for your specific customer and they will love this.

Sales

Selling, on the other hand is about persuading customers to buy your products by helping them believe it is what they are looking for. This will take place once the marketing has influenced a customer's buying habit.

After you have completed your customer focused marketing, you introduce your product or service to your potential customer, by highlighting the features as benefits for them.

This might include the following;

- advertising and promotion;

- direct selling; and

- supporting literature.

Once you have effectively shared the benefits of your product and service to your potential customer through marketing your brand, you can engage with them through your sales process to the point of purchase. Marketing and sales go hand in hand because of this simple, but critical-to-get-right process.

Here are two examples. One is a product driven and one a service driven business.

Product Driven Business, for example, building a product led brand.

The fashion industry is synonymous for having two seasons; spring/summer, autumn/winter. Having worked in the retail industry for more than 23 years, I always come across the same problem. For a brand to get into the marketplace it must first invest in stock. This stock has a short life cycle because of the two seasons. Whilst you can discount your stock it has an affect on your P/L (profit and loss) at the end of the year. The first route to market is having a business model, which allows you to get forward orders on your stock at a wholesale price before the stock even arrives in your warehouse. You need an online store allowing you to sell at the RRP (recommended retail price), which offers you, the business owner, a massive margin from cost to sale price.

Your other route to market is selling direct to the customer through your website and potentially, pop-up shops and market stalls in specific locations. By selling direct to the customer, the value you bring is focused on your brand, the quality of the product, the personal service you offer and the fact that they are part of a community of customers who love your brand. The consumer wants to feel good about buying your product. The customer has no interest in making money from your product, not like your other route to market; your business owner.

These two routes to market have a different type of target customer and therefore, the value that you give to those target customers has to be different. What do I mean by this? You're a brand who wants to sell into a high street store. The high street store has enough stock to last a season and it will buy various sizes and colours from your range, potentially spending ££££s with you at a wholesale price. This guarantees volume but does not guarantee a high margin. To achieve this, you might have to go to trade shows, travel and work with a distributor/agent to sell your products on your behalf and you may have to supply points of sale to help promote your brand in-store. More importantly, you are selling your product to the owner of the shop who knows their customer and knows they can make money from your brand. The value you bring to this target customer is the fact that you make them money.

Service Driven Business

There are many service driven companies, which sell direct to customers and sell direct to business. If you are a service driven business, you need to consider acquiring your customers through more than one sales avenue.

For example: if you are a consultancy firm specialising in sales, you need to think about more than one way of acquiring a customer to maximise the value you bring to a business, ultimately acquiring more customers and building your business. The more traditional way of acquiring a customer is going and sharing the value of your business with them. That person needs to see the value of what your business can do for them and they hire you to deliver that specific piece of work. Again, that individual is looking for personal service, potentially looking to have their hand held throughout the process and for knowledge sharing, to ultimately help them up-skill their own strengths.

The other Go to Market Strategy for a service driven business is to find organisations, which I call, channel partners, which already have your target customer on their database. You work with that organisation to share the benefit of your services to their customers.

The value proposition to the channel partner is that they are on a commission for every one of their target customers who buy into your business. Also, they know if your business delivers for their target customer, their customers will always remember them for making the introduction.

Ultimately, you must always be thinking about ways to bring different revenues into your business. This determines your business model and how you market your business online.

Always **Think #Digital First** and to get the most from your strategy, you must be laser focused on knowing your target customer (as mentioned in Chapter Two). Knowing their age, sex, income level, habits, interests, who they are and where they hang out, will help you understand their buying patterns.

Your timing is crucial in making sure the content you provide is current, adds value and contributes to the buyers' purchasing journey. As mentioned in Chapter Three, your buyers will go through the following process.

1. Build trust
2. Engage
3. Convert
4. Keep buying and became brand advocates

Building your brand's online presence offers twice the potential of acquiring a customer when you follow this four-step process.

Your 90-day Go to Market Strategy might look like this.

	30 DAYS	60 DAYS	90 DAYS
PEOPLE	What do we want to achieve?	Connect with decision makers on social networks	Send quotes & contract
PEOPLE	Who is going to implement	Build relationships	Implement retention strategy
PEOPLE	Branding yourself	Strategic hire	Expand the team
PROCESS	Key performance indicators	Implement & analyse	Take action
PROCESS	Budget	Extra costs?	What's the cost per lead?
PROCESS	Learn the technology	Other alternatives	Monitor & refine
TECHNOLOGY	Website	Work the issue	Get extra IT support
TECHNOLOGY	Content plan	Set IT goals	Measure & follow up
TECHNOLOGY	Tools to automate the message	Realign & stop what's not working	Stop & start the loop again

1 – 30 days: Research and set goals
30 – 60 days: Develop the plan and start the execution
60 – 90 days: Follow up and analyse

By having a 90-day Go to Market Strategy, with a focus on sales and marketing, you will be able to keep the business moving forward, while holding the team member personally accountable for each of the actions needed.

You role is to constantly be working on the business and not in the business, meaning you are not involved in the day-to-day operations of the business. As the business owner, you need to know, how you can take your business to the next level by implementing systems and procedures which enable the business to run smoothly and have the strategy that is always growing the brand awareness and increasing sales. This can only be done by taking a helicopter view of your business, your competitors and your industry; as things are always evolving, especially with the fast pace of technology, which is changing the way we work.

Marketing Plan

While it's important to know what's happening during the year in your business, for me 90 days has always been the perfect time to prepare, implement and measure, to a real effect. Measuring one year after a campaign has finished will not have any effect on where your business is right now.

Your 90-day Marketing Plan will explain what your marketing strategy is and how it will be executed to generate increased brand awareness and drive targeted traffic into your sales process. When developing your Marketing Plan you will need to ask yourself the following questions.

· How will you share your product/service?

· How will you entice potential customers to buy your product/service?

· How will you develop customer loyalty to develop repeat business and referrals?

Your Marketing Plan is created for your specific target audience, which you have already identified. Keep reading to find out what you can include in your 90-day Marketing Plan.

90-Day Plan

The visual on the next page is an example of a 90-day Marketing Plan, which includes what and when your business is going to market to your specific target audience. This template has a variety of offline and online marketing actions associated to a specific month. These actions and the month they happen will differ according to your business and the things you need to take into consideration before putting this plan together.

To help you, I've listed things you might want to think about;

· What time of year is your product mentioned online?

· When does your industry have a tradeshow?

· When are you launching a new product/service?

· Press Releases

· Industry Awards

· Channel Partner events

· Seasons; autumn/winter or spring/summer

· Competitions

· Networking events

MARKETING ACTION PLAN				
TARGET				
ACTIVITY	ACTION	Jun-14	Jul-14	Aug-14
Blog	West Essex Fashion Fair			
Ideas: clothes, country, events, local	Launch of New Top			
	Swimwear launch			
	*New Brand			
	Tour de France			
	Sale			
	Competition			
Newsletters	New in (Brands)			
	Launch of New Top			
	Swimwear			
	Sale			
	Competition			
Competitions	It's all about ME			
	Swimwear Giveaway			
	New Mums to be			
	Leather Jackets			
Sale	Summer Stock			
	Winter Stock			
SEO	Whats New			
	Dresses			
	Knitwear			
	Tops			
	Jackets			
	Trousers			
	Accessories			
	Brands			
Clothes Parties	Boutique X			
	Arbonne			
	Jamie at Home			
	Avon			

The download is colour-coded to help you stay focused on that specific action required in a particular month.

Now you've decided what actions you're going to take during the next 90-days, let's define what content you're going to share, using various tools and marketing platforms, with my 7-day Content Media Marketing Plan.

As mentioned in Chapter Four, content marketing is the sharing of media and published content to reach more customers as part of the customer acquisition journey and to increase your sales. This includes; everything from products, news, blogs, PR, videos, white papers, e-books, infographics, case studies and images, all of which can be shared across multiple channels with keywords in every message you share. This will come from the original SEO research document you prepared about the business in Chapter Four.

7-day Social Media and Content Marketing Plan
By following this step-by-step process, you will be able to manage all your social media in just 30 minutes a day and share all of your valuable content to your target audience knowing that every tweet, blog title and Pinterest post has been designed to connect with your customer.

"DO YOUR SOCIAL MEDIA
in
30 MINUTES A DAY "

It will take you one hour to prepare and amplify seven day's worth of content to all your social media and digital channels, as well as spending just a few minutes each day to have two-way conversations, find more followers and analyse the success.

From a best practice perspective, I recommend the following:

- 5 tweets a day
- 1 post a day in Facebook, Instagram, Pinterest and Google+
- 1 blog a week

For me, one tweet at two-hour intervals from 9am-5pm, once you've spent time analysing your online audience, will give you:

➜ 9am
➜ 11am
➜ 1pm
➜ 3pm
➜ 5pm

Pinterest infographics are a great source of data for your industry. By typing in the keywords of your industry and doing #infographic will give you the visual data around the best times to post. This is a great starting point but you can still analyse it for your business and your laser focused target customer and tweak accordingly.

" POTENTIAL ONLINE CUSTOMERS
——— *are touched by a brand* ———
8 TIMES BEFORE PURCHASING "

Every tweet must only be 100 to 120 characters including the shortened URL, based on the following strategy;

- 1st tweet of day is to be about your product/service
- 2nd tweet about your blog of the week
- 3rd tweet is company news

(new product/service coming soon/preview, an event, competition, press release, product on sale, new store, new product, trivia, behind the scenes, what is happening with the team, team challenges, testimonials, events, pictures of staff, old blog (if run out of content).

- 4th tweet another product/service
- 5th tweet global news i.e. news outside of the business

E.g. charity or upcoming events, whitepapers, best practice, blog or video interviews.

For Facebook, Pinterest, Instagram and Google+, you should only post once a day using the same content taken from tweets;

- Fri - blog of the week, competition announcement (when it happens, takes precedence)
- Sat - product/service
- Sun - company information
- Mon - staff at work, profile, trips etc
- Tue - global news

- Wed - another product/service or new product/service coming soon (carrot dangling)
- Thu - focus on a customer, thanking them for their referral or recommendation.

Hashtags– for use across all of your social networks;

- Location

#London | #UK | #Shoreditch

- Brand

#Google | #Asos | #Hootsuite

- Product/Service

#Swimwear | #CRM | #Email

- Target Customer

#Entrepreneur | #Female | #Foodie

Now you know what subject to talk about and when to post across which network, it's time to gather the information in a simple and easy to use document.

7 DAY SOCIAL MEDIA PLAN

DAY 1 (OF 7)	HR 1 - 0900 UK	HR 2 - 1100 UK	HR 3 - 1300 UK	HR 4 - 1500 UK	HR 5 - 1700 UK
TWITTER + LINKEDIN	WK Blog Thank you @e_nation for including me as a Top 10 Business Advisor http://ow.ly/IgNir #BusinessGrowth	Visual Quote Social Media Picture Quote of the Day - http://ow.ly/i/8sRjP #SocialMedia #Marketing	WK News Did you know @wvrknight will be talking at @PSAUK on the 22/3 about #Socialmedia #digitalmarketing	WK Blog #Hootsuite Review: 7 Features You Need to Use http://ow.ly/ #Technology	Education tweet How To Create Headlines That Get Clicks #Infographic - http://ow.ly/IgQKa
FACEBOOK		Take the latest WK blog on www.warrenknight.co.uk/blog and use above hashtags when suitable (no more than 2)			
PINTEREST + INSTAGRAM Important # Same format as Twitter		Take WK blog and add to "Blogs" board with picture			
G+ Important # Same format as Facebook		Post as you would on Facebook			

(Download from **Thinkdigitalfirst.today**.) Once you have filled in seven days of content, which will take only one hour, use Hootsuite to schedule to Twitter, Facebook, LinkedIn and Google+.

You can schedule using ScheduGram for Instagram, Viralwoot for Pinterest (as mentioned in Chapter Five).

90-day Sales Plan

The 90-day Sales Plan is the final part of the jigsaw for building a socially-savvy-business. It should be short, to the point and determine what the strategy should be and which tactics will be used to achieve the financial goals.

When thinking about sales for any size business, you only have to think of three things;

1. How do I get new customers?

2. How can I upsell and/or cross sell?

3. How can I retain clients?

To simplify the process even more, here are some quick tips to help you devise your Sales Plan.

Set simple and achievable goals on a daily basis.

· Make five cold calls

· Send 10 emails to introduce yourself and the business

· Arrange two face to face meetings

· Create no less than two proposals

· Make no less than two presentations

· Run one webinar (might only be monthly)

· Speak at one event (start with one a month)

You can download my simple 5-day spreadsheet to help you track and analyse the results and remember to always input the data into your CRM (as mentioned in Chapter Five).

	Monday	Tuesday	Wednesday	Thursday	Friday
Touch Base Calls					
Total per day	11	4	3	9	5
Client Calls - 2 per day					
Call 1	Call John S	Call James W	Call Daryl W	Call Patrice H	
Call 2	Call Sarah H	Call Chris G		Call Karl P	
		Call Jane M			
Meetings - 1 per day					
Meeting 1	Meeting with ASOS		Meeting GA	Breakfast meeting	Meeting Ryan
Meeting 2			Meeting with Innovate Centre	Meeting with Post Office	Meeting Oak
Meeting 3					Meeting Relish
Events		Launch party			
Seminars	Speak				Google campus
5 day meeting targets	2	2	2	2	2
Actual (over next 5 days)	3	1	1	2	3
Needed / Surplus	1	-1	-1	0	1

It can be difficult to find the right person to speak to if you are dealing with a company where you get held up by a gatekeeper. A gatekeeper is someone who is the first person to pick up an office phone and who screens all the calls for the decision maker. You need to find out who the key decision maker is, have your sales pitch ready and be as polite as possible when trying to reach that person. Gatekeepers know they hold a lot of responsibility and take that with pride so unless you know exactly why you want to speak to someone, they won't connect you.

Once you get past the gatekeeper, you can speak to the right person on the phone. Don't waste their time or yours, after you've built rapport, get straight to the point of the call and spend no longer than 30 minutes on this call.

If making calls is something you do not enjoy doing, here is a step-by-step structure to help you stay in control of the conversation and make sure you are helping the caller at each stage of the process and make sure you are always getting the results they want.

Stage 1

- Introduce yourself
- Build rapport

Stage 2

Pre-frame:
- 30 minutes for this call
- Find out what you can about them
- Answer their questions to get the results you want
- At the end of the call, how you are going to move forward, together

Stage 3

- Tell me about yourself
- Tell me about your business

What is your main driver for success? Is it your family? Money? Freedom? Want to succeed? And, what's your vision for the business?

Stage 4 - What they Want

Go back to difficulty - Ask for more feedback:
- Why is that?
- Explain more?
- Can you elaborate on that for me please?
- What do you mean?
- Why is that important? Rate on a scale of 1 - 10
- What are the barriers?
- Go into more depth (about key words mentioned)
- How important is that to you, on a scale of 1-10? – so I can get the idea
- Am I right in saying, you want more traffic from Facebook? (example) Explain process -How you see it.
- Small amount first - Make them see the problem

What concerns you the most: Time? Money? Or certainty?

Play it back again: Is it the time you don't have to spend on this? Is it to shorten the time to get to where you want to be. You are missing out on money, by not taking action now.

Stage 5

In a perfect world, what would you want to happen and: how much would you pay for that?

Stage 6

Pre-close:
- How do you feel things are going?
- Do you think we can work together?
- Do you have any other reservations?
- Did I understand YOU?

This is where you need to understand each other. At the end of the call what's the next step?

Moving Forward

At the end of your call, you should schedule a meeting to discuss your proposition further. This can either be at your office, or a mutual location agreed by you and the potential customer. You should have your objectives and a plan of what you want to talk about in that meeting. You need to be as engaging as possible otherwise your sales process will stop here.

Achieving customer buy in for your brand is essentially asking them to buy into you as well. You are representing your business and your passion needs to shine through. There is only one of you and that alone makes you unique. Make sure your business shares the same uniqueness.

Implement the strategy to get new customers

Now I'm going to let you into some of the secrets I use in the sales and marketing process that has enabled me to grow one of my companies to £1 million in less than two years. Also, I will share my knowledge about becoming the UK's Top 10 SME Superhero coach and the UK's Top 10 business advisor for 2015.

Here is an example of my customer acquisition journey, which I have mentioned a few times in this book. This example includes the marketing actions and the sales process all in one sheet.

There are two key things to remember when designing your journey:

1. Make sure you add every step to acquiring the customer all the way to really understand the time it takes; and
2. Always make a note of what works and what doesn't work.

This will help you avoid making the same mistake again and build good habits for your sales process.

Here are seven tactics I have used. Remember, these strategies are designed to capture new customers and gain market share.

1. Analyse your competitors

Taking a holistic overview of your competitive space and analysing the data keeps you one step ahead of the game, especially if a competitor has shifted their proposition to be very similar to yours. This is done by looking at your competitors' websites, social media activity (especially the directors or CEO on LinkedIn) and their ranking on Alexa. See if the business has grown or shrunk by checking their company accounts using Duedil and business information on Crunchbase. This will give you the granular research you need to create a comparison document and also an insight into how your competition utilises their online space.

2. Research: always have content to share

Sign up to Feedly (https://feedly.com/) and research the websites.

- Look for various industry websites and blogs using the search functionality and add them to a category for future reference; and
- Take the url of a website and add to Feedly 'Add Content' button and add them to a category for future reference.

Here are some websites for you to get started - I typed in eCommerce blogs:

- http://www.getelastic.com
- http://tamebay.com
- http://www.ecommercetimes.com
- http://ecommercepulse.com

3. Going to a networking event
Acquiring a new customer using technology and old school ways is powerful. Here is my tactic based on going to an event when I know a channel partner will be there.

1. Connect on all social networks
2. Say hi in LinkedIn before the event
3. Meet and build rapport, get business card
4. Send email to say hi and offer digital download
5. The download is a series of autoresponders
6. Track open rate
7. Call at touch point of opening a specific email
8. Arrange a meeting
9. Follow up and close

4. Twitter Growth Strategy
Find a Twitter account, which contains your target audience, and do the following.

1. Follow 15 people per day
2. Write a personal tweet to three of the people you've followed and send a link to the event or added value content, like a blog, article or press release
3. Do this five times a day, so now all 15 people have been contacted
4. Track who follows you, replies and signs up
5. If you get a sign up, follow up with a personal email
6. Follow up with a call
7. Arrange a meeting
8. Close as a new customer

Listening to what your industry or competitors are saying is just as important as pushing content out to your target audience.

5. Emailing customers using Pinterest website
Use social networks to find your customers.

1. Set up an event on Eventbrite or run a Google Hangout on Google+
2. Promote it on all social networks
3. Upload an image into Pinterest, in a suitable board
4. Edit the pin and add all the @name you are following and click 'Save'. Pinterest will email all the people saying they have been mentioned
5. Go back in remove the @... @...
6. Wait for people to sign up

Remember: You need to follow the person for this to work.

6. Selling to new Channel Partners
This has been one of the best tactics I've implemented to make sure I always have a pipeline of new customers.

1. Get your Personal or Admin Assistant or Virtual Assistant to collate a list of companies which have your target audience and include the decision maker's name, email, telephone number, company website and all social media accounts.
2. Input the name and email address into an email-marketing tool like Mailchimp and send a laser targeted email to the list.
3. Three days later look at the analytics and see who has opened the email, it will tell you who and how many times.
4. Now you know who is interested in what you have to say, go and find them across their social media platforms and Like, Follow and Share some information, so again, your brand is visible to them.
5. Pick up the phone and take them through your sales structure, which I explained earlier in this chapter.

This gives you the opportunity to contact the low hanging fruit of companies which four days ago might have never heard of you. Now they've received an email, a re-tweet, and a phone call. However, you have only focused on the companies, which have shown an interest and this data came from the open rate in Mailchimp, saving you time and making sure you are getting a good ROI (Return on Investment) on your time.

7. Getting Referrals

Within 30 days of delivering my product/service or solution, I will ask each of my new customers for at least three names and phone numbers of someone they know who may have a use for my product/service and solutions. Ask for a recommendation on LinkedIn and confirm if it's ok to publish it on your website.

These are just a few of my personal tactics that have helped me find targeted customers, build trust, engage and drive traffic to acquire leads and get sales. You might need to tweak them for your specific business, but trust me they work!

SEVEN

CUSTOMER RETENTION THROUGH LOYALTY

#WALKTHISWAY

"MAINTAINING BRAND LOYALTY
can be one of your
BIGGEST PROBLEMS "

Customer loyalty should be at the forefront of your customer retention strategy #WalkThisWay. Your new socially-savvy business will now be working with your customers daily, through sharing, added-value content, designed to help your company get noticed across the new social web. This includes everything from Google, Bing, Yahoo (SEO) through to Twitter, Pinterest, Facebook, Instagram, YouTube and Google+ (SMO).

You've now optimised your content so it's search-friendly and adds real value and explains how you help your customers by sharing content on a daily, weekly and monthly basis. By continuously sharing this content, you are automatically building loyalty with your customers and you are continuously focusing on your brand awareness and gaining market share.

As previously mentioned, for your target market to convert to being a customer, your business might have to touch them up to eight times. Once they become a customer, they will want to share the added value content with their community, ultimately becoming a brand advocate and loyal customer for your business.

As a business, you need to be continuously innovating and taking action to retain customers through loyalty. Before you can understand the strategies for this, you should know that 68% of consumers stop purchasing from a business because they are unhappy with the service they receive. The big question is: what are you doing to retain customers? Keep reading to find out the strategies I use to make sure my clients become more than just a one-time purchaser.

Set Expectations

From the get-go, make sure you set realistic expectations with your customers. I cannot stress the importance of this enough. It is better to under promise and over deliver than to set an expectation with your clients, knowing you will have a hard time delivering on that promise. This will allow you to eliminate uncertainty and help you to ensure your client's happiness on delivery of a product or service.

A customer is more likely to remember a negative experience and share this with their community. Say you over deliver on a service or product a number of times with the same customer and under deliver just once; this is what they will remember and ultimately, be their reason for terminating a contract or choosing a competitor to purchase products from.

Be the expert they need

"IT TAKES 10,000 HOURS to be an EXPERT"

One thing I pride myself on, is being as knowledgeable as possible so when a client starts working with me, I can offer them what they are looking for and nothing less. Regardless of what industry you are in, if you can be seen as an expert, this will help you retain your customers. Why; because people are scared of what they don't know.

Being an expert means that you have spent years perfecting your product or service so that customer loyalty becomes a natural step in the right direction for your business. Be the entrepreneur that your customers rely on, trust and recognise as an individual with a successful business.

As someone who has worked in sales, marketing and technology for more than 25 years, I am proud to say, I am an expert in those three fields and because of this, I have been able to retain customers and pick up new ones based on recommendations and loyalty.

Build relationships that lead to trust online and offline

As I have said, business is built on trust and loyalty and these are two of the biggest reasons a consumer will purchase a product or service on more than one occasion. Trust is an essential part of building relationships, especially through shared values in a service driven environment.

When you are working with a channel partner shared values means showing your interest in your client and their business. Understand the role you play in helping their business grow, while building a working relationship through loyalty at the same time.

Let's face it; your customers are online. They are glued to their computer screens and are using the latest social networks. Part of building a relationship, is giving you a strong social media presence that they can interact with. Why; because it's what they want to do.

"71% OF CONSUMERS
—have ended their relationship—
WITH A COMPANY DUE TO POOR CUSTOMER SERVICE "

Anticipate customer service issues

Be proactive and deal with issues around customer service before they even arise. Remember not to wait for something to happen, put a plan into action to eliminate any problems, before they become a roadblock to retaining a customer. Using Zopim, a live chat tool, which I spoke about in Chapter Five, is a great piece of functionality to use as part of your customer retention strategy.

For example, a major airline will text a customer to advise them of flight delays, avoiding any issues around them not being aware of this. As an entrepreneur, you need to put yourself in the customers' shoes. Take a proactive approach to what could become a negative experience.

Automation

Automation is an online form of a repeatable process which, when done right can leave you meeting your deadlines leading to an increase in customer loyalty and improved customer retention rates.

You should know from Chapter Three which tasks are going to be time-consuming for you and from Chapter Five which tools to use to help you with this. Customer retention using online automated messages is a way you can leverage your business, without having to take constant action to add value and retain loyal customers.

For example, I use Mailchimp as part of my email marketing strategy and customer retention strategy. I have a complimentary seven-day eCourse on one of my websites. Mailchimp's automation tool allows me to set up an email to go out to someone who signs up for that eCourse every single day, for the duration of the course. I only had to do this once and the rest was done for me. As soon as someone enters in their email address to access the course, it goes into Mailchimp and becomes a part of the autoresponder campaign. Part of this journey is to offer even more added value during a further 21-day period, where six more emails are automatically scheduled to go out to them.

"BUILD BRAND
— *loyalty* —
THROUGH POP-UPS "

Another way to build online loyalty is through pop-up windows from Wishpond. As I mentioned in Chapter Five, Wishpond is an email marketing tool, which also allows you to create landing pages, contests, promotions, forms, pop-ups and advertisements. Their website pop-up tool comes in five different formats; entrance; exit; timed; scroll; and click.

Build KPIs (Key Performance Indicators)

As I have said, 68% of customers stop purchasing from a company because they are unhappy with the service they are receiving. Improving customer service will ultimately boost how many customers you retain.

Establish your SMART KPIs; Specific, Measurable, Achievable, Relevant and Time-based. This helps you understand what is stopping you from improving your customer retention and how you can improve this.

Throughout this book, I have shared with you SMART KPIs. Until now, I haven't framed them as SMART KPIs because I've wanted to stay away from this terminology. For these words to have meaning, I wanted to give you relatable, real-life examples.

Go above and beyond

Your customers expect you to go above and beyond, as they know what loyalty means to businesses. Take a mobile phone service provider for example. When you call them to upgrade your phone, you expect to not have your contract fee increased and not pay a single penny for the handset. This can be difficult but as soon as you play the loyalty card, they will go above and beyond to make sure you are getting the deal you deserve and they get you for at least another 18 months as a returning customer.

Feedback Surveys

Customer feedback surveys are one of the best ways to show your customers that you are listening to what they have to say and want to improve the service you offer them. This is invaluable for learning your customers' expectations. I shared a great survey tool called SurveyMonkey in Chapter Five. However, Google also have a great application, where you can create your own survey and send the link to customers.

There are three different metrics you should be monitoring through your surveys.

1. Individual Responses

Look at individual responses because understanding the bigger picture of what all customers say collectively will not help you solve a particular issue.

2. Ongoing Feedback

To track feedback, you need to do more than one survey. During a period of time, you can see exactly what areas have improved and which haven't.

3. Knowing Your Strengths and Weaknesses

This feedback will provide you with the intelligence you need to make improvements around your weaknesses, while making your strengths, stronger. This will help you retain customers because real data-driven feedback is what will make your business grow.

Shopping Cart Abandonment

Have you ever followed one of your customers' journey through Google Analytics real time and seen that they have got to the payment page and then left your page? You don't need to see it happen, to know that it definitely is happening. The average shopping cart abandonment rate for eCommerce is an astounding 65 - 75%, as much as 95% on mobile. This means that you are losing a large amount of business and unfortunately, even the best shopping cart solutions can't find a guaranteed fix.

VE interactive is a great online tool to help you optimise the purchase journey on your website, ultimately reducing your shopping cart abandonment.

However, there are steps you can take to ensure you are doing everything to reduce that 65% for your business.

1. Free shipping;
2. Simplify the checkout process;
3. One-click payment;
4. Get rid of hidden charges; and
5. Offer real time support.

Google is Your Friend

Google is a business's best friend. I found this out when they mentioned me in a Google+ post, on their official Google Analytics page to more than 3.3 million followers. What better brand advocate can you get? This wouldn't have happened, if I wasn't blogging on a regular basis about relevant and interesting content. Blogging is a key part of your marketing strategy, which I spoke about in Chapter Six.

Let's move on to a very important part of understanding where your customers are coming from, when they are leaving and how you can make it easier for them to use and stay on your website. I previously mentioned Google Analytics as a tool in Chapter Five. Here is a guide to helping you use it for your business.

1. Adding the Code

Once you have set up your account on Google Analytics, you will need to add the code they give you, into the back end of your website. This is so you can accurately track all activity.

2. Knowing What You Can Measure

After you have inputted the code, click on 'view report' on the screen, which will bring you to the main dashboard. There are various types of data you can measure which includes; visitors, traffic sources, content, goals and eCommerce. What you track, depends on what you want to achieve.

3. Setting Up Your Dashboard

There is a main dashboard where you will see an overview of your data. This is customisable. You can chose to see any of your reports from this area and also more detail around each report, click 'view report'.

4. Adjusting the Time Range

Google Analytics will by default give you your results based on a month-long period. You can change this by adjusting the date range.

Here are three specific dashboards for your business, focusing on social media, lead generation and eCommerce which I spoke about in Chapter Five. These are completely free of charge and are an essential part of knowing where you need to improve your online presence to help retain customers.

As well as the tools above, you can use Hootsuite to manage your social media analytics. Hootsuite allows you to combine real-time social actions taking place around your networks with an engagement solution, giving you access to data, which you can take immediate action on.

This tool allows you to;

- track your brand growth;

- visualise social demographics;

- measure sentiment metrics;

- identify social influencers;

- see what content resonates; and

- create detailed social reports.

Make it Personal

It is crucial when building a social-savvy business that you make every action you take around your customer as personable as possible. When sending a survey to your customers, get their date of birth so you can send a special discount/gift and written card on their birthday. It will be an unexpected, but very much appreciated, surprise.

With every order you receive, if you're a product driven business, send a personal, handwritten message so your customer knows you appreciate their purchase.

From making a good first impression to tailored emails, personalisation and mobile customisation, you are making sure that your customers know what they want and that their needs come first.

IN SUMMARY

You are the person in charge of your businesses success or failure. By reading **Think #Digital First** you have been guided through a step-by-step process to change your business mind set. I have shared with you: how to manage your time; how to stay up to date with the latest tools and technology; and how to increase your productivity for fast growth.

Building your framework for success is an integral part of business growth. This book can help you do this by following the step-by-step process. The strategies and techniques I have shared are packed full of great tools, which demystify the new digital age and build your entrepreneurial footprint online.

You are now ready to find and market to your target customer, build your Go to Market Strategy and retain customers through implementing loyalty.

My role is to help you grow your business and everything in this book is going to be available on my website. Come and speak to me on social media, via email or in person at one of my keynote seminars, or attend one of my webinars. The seven steps I have taken you through may leave you feeling overwhelmed but I am easily accessible to help you and everything we discuss is in complete confidence.

I have shared my business experiences and have written this book from the heart. I hope that what I have shared will fast track you through the mind field of starting, or growing your successful business.